I0116497

Journey to My Past Lives
12 Reincarnation Stories Retrieved by Hypnotherapy Method

Nathalia Sunaidi

© Nathalia Institute Publishing

ISBN 978-979-19811-2-5

"This book is rather controversial. Not everyone—perhaps only a few people—can understand, or even accept Nathalia's way of thinking. Somehow, this book plays with our mind and encourages us to search for an answer to the question: "Who Am I?" —**Andy F. Noya, Metro TV, Chief Editor and Kick Andy Host**

"Past life adventures are not easy to understand and nor are they experienced by everyone. However, that doesn't mean that a past life doesn't exist. Knowing information about past lives can be helpful. However, it is far more important if that knowledge can be used as a learning experience tool to step up to achieve success in the future. Keep your heart open and your soul pure when reading *Journey to My Past Lives*, to increase your knowledge and to see a positive impact from Nathalia's extraordinary past experiences."—**Andrie Wongso, Motivator and best-selling author**

"Windows that open every now and then to past or future lives should be marked as elements that enrich our today spiritual lives. We are not bound by those lives, but can learn from them. Nathalia's exploration into these lives proves that time is actually circuitous and that those circulations are an illusion that makes games named Lives applies."—**Dewi Lestari, "Supernova" serial writer**

"I found impressive things. Entering the past can be an amazing experience, and it can yield a meaningful spiritual journey that strengthens and guides your mind to more fruitful directions."— **Ade Tri Marganingsih, Chief Editor, MATABACA**

"An extraordinary and valuable book that can increase our level of consciousness towards spiritual Enlightenment."—**Adi W. Gunawan, Re-educator, Mind Navigator, and best-selling author of *Hypnosis: The Art of Subconscious Communication.***

"Self discovery! Often our perspective about ourselves is totally different from another person's perspective about us. This book gives us guidance on how to know ourselves truly. The minute you surrender, you might find exactly what you seek. I highly recommend this book for your journey to find the purpose of your life."—**Alexandra Dewi, Managing Director, Sun Hope Indonesia; co-author of *I Beg Your Prada***

"Very interesting! Open the path to know our own potential."— **Andrea Hirata, author of the tetrology novel *Laskar Pelangi***

"Truthfully, every soul is growing and past lives complete the dynamic. A soul is an amazing growing substance."—**Gede Prama, author of 22 Inspirations Book**

"*Journey to My Past Lives* offers an extraordinary reading experience. Nathalia will take you on an adventure in your deepest and hidden lives' passages. Be ready!"—**Jessica Huwae, writer on Soulmate.com, and Managing Director of SPICE!**

"*Journey to My Past Lives* provides constructive and corrective reflections to increase the quality of your present life. You will be able to improve many things after watching this past lives video. Nathalia has written her interesting past lives in the form of a video transcript and her work conveys the single message: past lives do exist and are real. Explore your video with this guide book!"—**Ponijan Liaw, best-selling author of *The Art of Communication that Works* and co-writer *of Simplify Your Life with Zen***

Table of Contents

Acknowledgements

Many different people provided the support and assistance I needed to publish this book. These individuals encouraged me to write about my past lives' experiences and to assemble them into a book. Special thanks to Romy Rafael, who was willing to write my introduction. My gratitude also goes out to writers and publishers who sent in remarkable endorsements for my book. They are Andy F. Noya, Andrie Wongso, Ade Tri Marganingsih, Adi W.Gunawan, Alexandra Dewi, Andrea Hirata, Dewi Lestari, Gede Prama, Jessica Huwae, Ponijan Liaw, and Sumarsono Wuryadi.

I would also like to thank my regression clients and those willing to give testimony that enabled me to complete this book. They are Paulina, Lydia Anggariani, Alex Triadi, Joni, Cisca, and many others.

Thank you to Gunawan, my husband, who always encouraging me to pursue my dreams to write my stories and present them in a book. He has always encouraged me to be a hypnotherapist. Thank you, Gunawan, for being my best friend in this spiritual journey.

Furthermore, I would like to thank my parents, who love me sincerely and wonderfully, and Gunawan's parents, who provide moral support and put their trust in me. Thank you to all my best friends for your trust and support.

Thank you to my english editor, Amy, who has made this book more beautiful to read. Thank you for your guidance, suggestions, and experience sharing; you have given this book the ability to reach my readers.

Thank you to my readers who trust me to lead you to your own past life regression journey. And finally, thank you to everyone who has labored to help this book achieve publication.

Preface

What is past life regression?
Do you believe in reincarnation?
Do you believe that you were someone else?
Do you have previous life before your current life?
How can past life regression (PLR) guide you?

Many people over the world believe they have experienced reincarnation. And those reincarnation experiences have a positive impact that can be used as part of a healing process in therapy. Many people are searching for a path and way to know more about their previous life before their present life. So, this book pretty much will guide you to answer those complex questions above.

PLR—its literal definition—is a journey into past life. When you are hypnotized, you can track that period before your present life. What if you don't believe in past life regression? Even if you don't believe in reincarnation, most people believe that when we die, our soul will continue to live in a different live as a different person. Meaning that, after we die, our soul will continue to occupy a different body until that body or physical form also becomes old and an improper vessel for the soul.

If this happens, then the soul will leave the body and return by joining with a different body. And this circle will continue until the end of universe. According to the myths, this happens because the soul will continue to learn and develop in every new life it experiences. Ultimately, this happens so that the soul will continue to improve in each of its incarnations.

Maybe you read this book because you or people you know believe in a previous life. There is unique way to know your previous life through hypnotherapy. I suggest that you open your mind to this possibility and read Nathalia Sunaidi's book.

Romy Rafael
Hypnotherapist

Introduction

I first read about the past life regression method (PLR) in a book. That encounter inspired me to learn more about hypnotherapy and to study it seriously. When I attempted it for the first time, I failed to regress myself into my past life. In continued practicing and was ultimately about to enter my previous life and experience rich details from those experiences. I even eventualls learned to fast forward or replay time from that past life to explore more intricate details and lessons from those experiences.

When I first entered my previous life experience and experienced the clarity and details, I was not sure if it was really my past life or just my imagination. There were thousand of questions racing through my mind. If that previous life was only my imagination, why were the images so detailed? Why did I experiences such strong feelings about those moments?

If it was only my fantasy, why had I "chosen" a scenario as a fisherman who had been murdered—this was one of my previous life stories in Thailand. This fisherman had a regular life; he spent his days just plaiting fishnet and catching fish. Why didn't I "choose" a scenario as a princess who had married a prince charming?

Again, if it was only my imagination, why I did I have such an in-depth understanding of professions and skills that I have never learnt before? But if I had glimpsed my previous life, how could I learn more? Couldn't only religious people or holy scholars see and truly understand their past lives? How can it be that easy for me to view my past life?

I was confused. I should continue my practice and learn more, or just quit everything because it could be dangerous "insanity"?

I decided to demonstrate my past life regression in front of my best friends. I entered the trance condition and entered my three past lives periods: as a fisherman in Thailand, as a Dutch woman, and as a monk.

In my previous life in Thailand, I was a fisherman who was killed by another fisherman. I eventually discovered that the fisherman who had murdered me in my previous life was my best friend in my current life. He was even in the room with during this regression!

In my other previous life, I was a little girl in Holland, and my friends witnessed that during that regression, my personality changed completely. In my trance condition, once I had entered that past life, I acted and spoke like a little girl. At one point, I was crying and whining to get these special cinnamon cookies I wanted. When I was still in that past life regression, as that girl who had grown up and was near death, my voice became weak and I whispered like no energy left— just like the voice of an old lady who was dying.

When I entered my other past life, I was a monk who was just passing a village that had been massacred. All my best friends in the room were very frightened, because I was describing in detail how the women and children of that village had been massacred.

In my own current life, I have no skill as an actress. I cannot make up stories easily or play out stories with any convincing facial expressions or deep emotions. This had led me to believe that the past lives I've experienced are real. We just need to know the right way to enter them.

To support of what I believed, I began to do some research on PLR. I am a very logical person and I approached my research very methodically and rationally. I wanted to find evidence of the stories I'd learned in my past lives.

In one of my past lives, I was born as a Sundanese girl, and in that life, I speak Sundanese daily. As that Sundanese girl, I died of cassava poisoning when I was just twelve years old. When I came out of that trance, I remembered things I heard and said as that Sundanese girl.

I asked a couple of friends who understand Sundanese what those bits and pieces of language mean, but none of them knew the words. Maybe those words were from an ancient dialect of Sundanese?

It wasn't easy to figure out if what I had pictured in my visions was historically true. Sometimes the figures of year pictured in that moment is vague so there is big changes that it is invalid.

At that point, my belief in past life regression was shaken again. Even so, led by curiosity, I continued to explore past life regression. One day, I found a book about how to interpret past life stories. The author clearly stated that it was not necessary to find concrete evidence of the past life existence. Instead, the author explained, I could obtain all all the proof I needed simply by asking myself, "Are my visions of previous life experiences influencing my understanding and learning process in my current life?"

The main point was that if past lives give enlightenment and understanding, and they are true. That's the evidence of past life existence. It was a revelation! This concept was the consciousness foundation that I needed to understand more about my past life. This book made me realized that I had been moving in the wrong direction in seeking to understand my past life. I had spent lots of time and energy seeking verification and data that was difficult to find. As a result, I gradually forgot why I had originally sought out my past life, which was to experience a spiritual learning process, to increase my understanding and awareness, to make a positive impact on my life, and to promote healing to my current life.

Now, I believe that what I experienced were my past lives, because those past lives' experiences have given me healing and brought me to new understandings through lessons shown by those past moments.

This book contains 12 past life experience stories that I've chosen. I wrote my own questions and answers (Q&A). I choose this method because it's what happened when I gathered information through the *self-hypnosis* method in my past life regression.

I wrote this book hoping to share my experience. Not just to share about my past life experience, but also to share the understanding and awareness that I gathered from my dialog result with the *superconscious mind*. I believe there are many valuable and universal life lessons that we can learn from past life regression.

Entering past lives' experiences can be a remarkable and meaningful spiritual journey. It is a journey that can heal us and others. I hope this book will be useful for all of us.

Theory

Past Life Regression is one of therapy methods that can increase human quality of life, through a series of long life journeys. Until now, PLR was applicable through hypnotherapy. Freud pioneered this theory in his research into bringing the *subconscious mind* to the *conscious mind* to heal it. It means that by knowing the cause of different symptom or problems that occur, a person will experience healing moment.

Through his different experiments, Freud rediscovered his childhood trauma and was able to bring that experience to a healing process in himself. Freud's technique dragged the subject to the moment of trauma and brings back that trauma again as *therapeutic* method; this concept drew harsh criticism from his peers. They declared that the painful memory experienced again by the subject was just fantasy. The method that used to deliver a subject to its own childhood was hypnosis method—considered taboo at that time.

In year 1927, Paul Brunton wrote about a technique that had been developed by a yogi to enter past lives. A Buddhist monk explained to Brunton that he practiced meditation on a daily basis and endeavored to enter past lives as taught by Buddha. That monk practiced by entering his past moment few days ago, then few weeks ago, few months ago, few years ago, until as far as the birth moment, and finally he was able to step back to his previous life. Brunton felt that this method, however effective, took too long to be implemented.

Before 1970, entering past lives was considered part of psychic or paranormal activities because it was very hard to access past lives and only few could do it—seemingly only psychics and paranormal specialists.

Jung's *active imagination* method, however, influenced transformation techniques in therapy world. In 1920, only a few academics knews of Carl Jung. But by 1970, Jung's theory had become the root of the imaginary method that began to gain acceptance in society. In 1960, regression usages to return to the childhood moment as a therapeutic method began to broaden. Out of that method, a lot of different accessible, but sophisticated hypnosis methods were discovered; a lot of subjects entered their past lives by using those methods.

In 1970, a lot of practicing psychologists were researching PLR. In 1978, Helen Wambach, a psychologist, was researching the artifacts, clothes, and cultures from another period of time. Her research appears in her famous book, *Reliving Past Lives*. Edith Fiore, a clinic psychologist and professional hypnotherapist, launched her famous book, You Have Been Here Before. Fiore entered her previous live when she was doing *age-regression,* and this was an experience was that against her beliefs. She reported that many of her clients entered their past lives. Strangely, the past live journeys have given them healing process towards her clients. Based on her findings, Fiore chose to focus on PLR.

Since then, PLR has been one of the standard hypnotherapy therapeutic methods and has been taught in many different institutes and hypnotherapy training courses.

Model of Mind

Our mind consists of three layers: *unconscious mind, subconscious mind,* and *conscious mind.* Every layer of the mind has its own function.

Functions of the conscious mind:

- Temporary memories
- Analysis
- Rationalizations
- Will power

Functions of the subconscious mind:

- Permanent memories
- Habits
- Emotions
- Self defense
- Homeostatic

Functions of the unconscious mind:

- Implementing automatic body functions: heart beats, breathing, etc.
- Regulate the body's immune system
- Storing memories from our past lives

Every function of those three layers of the mind is connected one another. Most people are only aware of the functions of the conscious mind. If we asked people to name the function of the mind, most people will list "thinking," (referring to the function of the mind that analyzes and rationalizes) or "remembering" (referring to the function of mind that stores temporary, short-term memories, because few people remember infancy or birth)

Our daily activities are always using this *conscious mind* function. But behind that system, our mind's process is very complicated, complex, and mysterious. Why mysterious? Because our research into the human mind has only uncovered a fraction of its potential. This mysteriousness makes me want to discover more about hypnotherapy because hypnotherapy teaches us how to enter another layer of our mind. Entering the *subconscious mind* or *unconscious mind* is like entering a time machine where we can travel to different time dimensions from the past and the future. We can glimpse everything that influences our present life.

How is our mind process this activity? To make it simple and clear, I will explain by using illustration of moments. Let's say you are driving a car. Suddenly your back tire explodes and your car becomes wobbly. What's on your mind? You know that your back tire has exploded so what do you do? You will choose to stop and change the tire with the spare.

The function of mind that enables you to identify that this explosion is your flat tire and think of a solution comes from the analysis and rationalization function of your *conscious mind.* However, behind that identification and decision making process is a series of mind processes that occur prior to the decision. When you hear the tire explosion and you feel your body shaking inside the car, your mind will search the database in your mind for similar incident—inside your subconscious mind. This series of incidents is called a flat tire. You know it because you entered data that matched up with data from a similar incident. Maybe it's from a pastexperience, people, story, or from watching TV. And if you don't have a past experience with a flat tire, your emotion is flat.

Then, your *solution database* in your *subconscious mind* tells you to change that flat tire. In this one situation, you are running a conscious mind function to analyze and rationalize the situation and you are simultaneously running a subconscious mind function by accessing your permanent memories, emotions, and habits about having a flat tire incident. You also access your unconscious mind when your body responds to the incident normally because you don't have a bad experience about having flat tire (if you did have a bad experience with a flat tire, then your unconscious mind will react with fear, and you will experience a faster heartbeat, etc.). And if you do a survey by asking few people about having flat tire, then you will get very different responses to the problem and the solution. Maybe someone would phone her husband to ask him to pick her up (I would take this solution), or someone else would continue driving to the nearest workshop, etc. That's because every person has a different *subconscious mind* that contains experiences from their past.

What if you have a flat tire and have a hysterical reaction, but don't know why? You just know that every time you hear an explosion from a flat tire, you feel a moment of terror that makes your heart beat fast, leaves you in cold sweat, and makes your whole body shake. If so, you need to know if there is any experience related to a flat tire incident inside your *subconscious mind* that is causing this reaction in your current life. Regression therapy helps you search past experiences in your *subconscious mind.* If you still can't find the cause, then PLR could be one of alternatives to expose it.

The whole life experience is recorded in our *subconscious mind.* It will be a whole life program, and we cannot change it. To explain it, let's look at the flat tire example again. After you implement regression therapy, you will find the causes of your terror. Perhaps you will find that in of your previous lives, you had an accident because of a flat tire. When it happens in your current life, the fear you felt in that experience finds you again. That moment of terror was recorded as a program: every time you hear a flat tire explosion, it will lead to frightening accident; your body will experience symptoms such as shaking, quickened heartbeat, and sweaty palms and feet. After exploring the moment deeper, you discover that the accident occurred because you were drunk and drove. From the cause and effect experience, you learn not to drink and drive in your current life. This new knowledge will replace the old memory in your *subconscious mind.* Since then, every time you experience flat tire, your *subconscious mind* will experience not the terror of that accident, but the lesson learned from it instead.

The homeostatic function in your *subconscious mind* makes programs in your *subconscious mind* that will not change unless we change them through discretion awareness. That is why we need a different type of contemplation method, therapy, and meditation—so that we can understand our past lives and apply those lessons in our current lives. I will explain these functions of mind plainly in my book about hypnosis and hypnotherapy.

Hypnotherapy and Past Life Regression

To be able to access our permanent memory storage, which resides in the *subconscious* and *unconscious minds*, we don't need to leave our *conscious mind.*

Between our *conscious mind* and *unconscious mind* (in this part, I am referring to the *subconscious mind* as part of the *unconscious mind),* there is *critical factor. Critical factor* is like a gate that opens and closes access into the *subconscious mind.*

Critical factor opens when our emotions (fear, sadness, happiness, etc.), relaxation, focus, and concentration come together through *repetition* and a *moment of belief.* To be able to access past lives' memories in our *subconscious mind*, we need to open our *critical factor* gate; this is the importance of hypnotherapy.

Hypnotherapy is a therapy that uses the hypnosis method. The definition of hypnosis is a process to open critical factor from *conscious mind* so that a person can enter his *subconscious mind.* So, hypnotherapy is a therapy that uses emotion, relaxation, focus, and concentration, repetition, or belief to access the *subconscious mind.* The PLR therapy uses the hypnotherapy method to access the *subconscious mind* so that we can access past life memories.

Journey of Consciousness

Life is a journey towards perfection. Every time we track this journey, we hope that it will lead us to our destination. There is a concept about essential that full of unconditional love, perfectionism, discretion, and eternity. These conditions are the final purpose of our long journey.

Life is a spiritual journey that drives every individual to seek more in life than what is possible in the material world. Every life chapter should able to deliver awareness that helps us get closer to perfection because that is the center of this long journey—to reach something absolute and spiritual. Every birth is a new chapter like a white blank sheet of paper. Because it's still pure, we can fill it with kindheartedness or evilness. The evilness will cause us to move further away from our God and the kindheartedness will move us closer. Just as a student must retake a class if he does not pass the exam, we must repeat every chapter of our lives until we learn from it.

If your life journey was written in a book, then that

biography of your different lives would be sizable because it would contain all your mistakes, success, carelessness, and discretions. Just as we can reread sections of books to highlighted important points as a lesson, PLR allow us to re-open our book of journey and learn from our mistakes.The consciousness that travels once had different names, bodies, and faces. And in every chapter of his lives have given discretion to be learned and deliberate.

Purposes of Past Life Regression

The purpose of PLR is to know about cause and effect law (karmic law). Learning and exploring karmic law is the basic purpose of PLR practice. Implementing PLR without revealing cause and effect is useless and pointless.

Every moment that happens in our life has cause. Although life often seems unfair, everything in this life is relatively fair in the scope of the big picture. Anyone can certainly feel unfairness in his life (sexual harassment, assault, poverty, etc.), but these unfair events are the punishments of life. Yes, these events are unfair if we just interpret them in the context of one chapter, but taken in the scope of our many lives, they might not be so. According to karmic law, someone will feel himself a victim from his previous lives if they caused him to be punished for what he's done in the past.

Awareness of the journey of life and death is called samsara. The consciousness will travel to many lives until it reaches perfection. During the journey, every deed is counted. Good or bad deeds that done by someone will lead to cause and effect for the future life.

PLR helps us understand our roles and what we have done in our past lives that can cause us to be a victim in our current life.

Repetitive Pattern

If we failed to complete our life lesson in a past life, the lesson will be repeated on the next life continuously until we find the solution.

This repetitive pattern causes suffering. This indicates that those patterns need to be changed. Repetitive patterns usually happen in relationship connections. Someone will continuously relate to or go through same pattern towards other people as long as the pattern does not change. For example, relationship connections that are filled with hate will repeat until one of these two sides breach it through a forgiving process and loving care.

A repetitive pattern process gives us the opportunity to correct our mistakes in the past life by doing good deeds. It also tells us about unfinished businesses so that we can finish those tasks and pass the test this time.

Chapter 1

The Life of Jing Un Master, Year 475

One day, I was in a bookstore and I stumbled across a book about reincarnation. The book was a compilation of one therapist's stories of Americans' past lives. In that moment, I felt very excited and very happy! I felt as if I had found something very valuable in my life. I read the book quickly. Every page I read made me more interested in hypnotherapy. I wanted to know more about this method—and especially about past lives, reincarnation, and methods to enter past lives. People know this method by the name of Past Life Regression (PLR).

I read every book I found about hypnotherapy. I practiced every method described for entering past lives. Soon thereafter, I learned how to enter my past lives by connecting with my *superconscious mind* and was even able to eventually see my *future lives*. My passion for this subject grows every day.

I began to practice my regression technique to help other people access their past lives. I took my best friend to his past lives and guided him to be connected to his *superconscious mind.* The result was amazing! We discovered that many changes happened in his life. My best friend thanks me for taking him into a spiritual journey inside his own mind. This spiritual journey has changed him and has helped him change into a better person.

Shortly afterwards, we decided to inform our best friends of this incredible experience. I took my closest friends, one by one, through their own experiences with their past lives through the hypnotherapy method. I witness for myself how they experienced their past lives' spiritual journey and took lessons from it. When I saw my best friends feeling happy and passionate, telling me their past lives' stories as a result of their connection with their *superconscious mind*, I realized the true power of giving.

If every person could see his past lives, realize that he has been trapped by the same problems again and again, and get connected with their *superconscious mind* to find an answer to all of the questions, they can enter to their future lives with the best options to grow and live happier lives.

Journeying through my past lives journey has been a very interesting experience, because it has taught me that we travel in our own mind. This spiritual journey will heal and revolutionize our mind, and we will remember the experience forever.

I will share my stories about the past lives' journey I have experienced. My past lives journey starts with a question: "What happened in my past lives to lead me to be interested in hypnotherapy in my present life?"

To make it easier for you to follow my journey, I will use Questions (Q) and Answers (A) method by using first-person language. This is my own past lives regression through the hypnosis method.

Q: Can you see yourself?
A: Yes. I am wearing coats and my head is bald. I am a monk.

Q: Where are you now?
A: In a temple

Q: Can you describe the temple to me?
A: The temple is located on top of mountain far away from local houses. The air is very cold.

Q: What is your name?
A: Sounds like Jing Un. My students call me Jing Un Master.

Q: Which country you are at now and what year?
A: China. Now is year 475. But, I'm not so sure.

Q: How long have you lived in this temple?
A: I have lived here since I was little. I really like my life here.

Q: Can you tell me about your daily activities?
A: Our duty is daily routines like sweeping the floor, cooking, and meditation practice. But now, I meditate more often.

Q: Let's move time forward to learn why you are very interested in hypnotherapy. What you are doing now?
A: I am sweeping the floor in the temple. Suddenly strong wind strikes and it becomes very dusty. I find myself thinking about a lot of creatures that do not know which way to go. They go round and round, repeating their lives over and over, and always losing direction. Just like dust that is blown by the wind in the air. They never notice that they have been going around and around with the same mistakes. I wonder if there is a way to find direction in the soul that could lead them and guide them when they are lost.

Q: So, what will you do?
A: Since then, I often meditate. I try to find ways to see my past lives and to be connected with my highest direction.

Q: Did you find your way?
A: After long process of learning and training, finally I succeeded. I guide my students to enter their past lives, so that they can learn mistakes they have repeated in the past, and then they can pass it.

Q: So, is this the thing that caused you to be very interested in hypnotherapy in your current life?

A: Yes, for a while I taught my students to see their past lives, and then I thought that if I can only teach and help students in this temple, it was very limited. If I could tell people outside the temple, I could help more people. That is why I insisted on being reborn as a regular person who would have the capability to see past lives and connect to that highest discretion. I am willing to guide other people in this task.

From that regression, I became mafhum, which is why I am very passionate about becoming a hypnotherapist. Then, I asked myself if anything else in my other past lives also gives me a strong passion for it.

Q: Can you see yourself?

A: Yes. I am wearing yellow cloth twisted around the private part of my body and a folded fabric on my head.

Q: Are you a man or a woman? How old are you?

A: A boy. I am twelve years old.

Q: Which country are you in now?

A: Namaskar City, India.

Q: What year?

A: Around the year 300.

Q: What are your daily activities?

A: I work as a farmer.

Q: Tell me about your life?

A: I live with my parents in a small wooden house in the middle of the field. I like meditating. Usually, I meditate at home, but if I need more peaceful situation, I will go to this cave on the hill.

Q: Now, let's move a couple of years forward to know what you've done in your life in that moment. What were you doing?
A: I was meditating in a cave. I live in that cave, but I can't focus on my meditation. I often feel bored and go outside to relax.

Q: Let's move forward a couple of years to see the biggest achievement in your life as a hermit. What did you see?
A: I am meditating in a cave.

Q: Are you any different since last time I asked?
A: Yes. I am thin, bearded, and I have long black curly hair.

Q: So, what were you doing?
A: I am jumping around happy.

Q: Why are you jumping around?
A: I am very happy because I finally understand the journey of soul that is reborn again and again to attain perfection. I want to share my experience with everyone.

Q: Do they accept it?
A: Yes. They accept it.

Q: What makes you think that they accept your comprehension?
A: I was sitting under the tree and teaching lots of people. I made them enter a trance and guided them to enter their past lives. After that, some of them felt very happy and enlightened. I realized that they accepted my lesson. Many sick people came to me. I told them to focus on their sickness, by pointing at the source of pain, and then I guided them to enter their past lives

that were the source of their pain.

Q: Is it working that way?
A: Yes. And they become enlightened and healed spiritually. Is not important if the sickness has cured or not. The most important thing is that they know the source of their pain and understand the lesson they get from the pain they suffer. It is too bad that I can only teach and heal men. A lot of women came to me to learn or asked to be healed, but because I am a monk, I cannot be with women.

Q: How will that take form in your current life?
A: Because, in my life as a monk, I determine my future life, I will be born as female so that I can help women who want to learn and so that I can heal them.

Q: Now, let's move forward to the final moment of your life as a monk. How's your dying process in the end of your life?
A: I saw myself old and dying. I left my body when I was sleeping on the wooden bed.

From that regression, I learned the power of determination. Determination does not know a time limit. A determination has been established, decided, and self committed and will be self commando to all of mind elements to implement that determination itself.

The way determination power works is similar to a manager who ordered every mind elements to be aware all the time and capture every opportunity to reach the dreams they have established.

The determination power will guide me in every step I make to find my past lives regression through the hypnosis method.

I don't know why I keep experiencing things that are

related closely to past lives regression and the hypnotherapy method. It was almost as if I was experiencing step-by-step guidance to become a hypnotherapist who specialized in past lives regression.

Without knowing it, I had already set my power of determination in my past lives, and it was guiding me to reach dreams that I had established in my past lives. This determination was to guide people to their previous lives and to connect them with their highest discretion.

"The power of determination that companies a dream will act like a commando that will order all elements of mind to fulfill that dream. How big is the power of determination! Have you planted a determination in your dream?"

Chapter 2

Marichzka's Forbidden Love

I have never understood why my mother and I cannot agree. I find it hard to share my thoughts with her because we always have totally different ways of thinking. Sometimes I feel that my mother always pushing me to do what she wants. If she's disagreeing with what I have done, she judges me by saying that I don't love her. I often fight with my mother and we always end our disagreements in high, tense voices.

Small misunderstanding between us can leads to big fight. I feel that my mother is fussy about small things—things I think unnecessary to be argued. Sometimes my mum's words trigger my emotions. Every time it happens, I feel sorry in the end for not controlling my emotions. Truly, I love my mother. She is my mother and I have no doubt that she dearly loves me too. We just have totally different ways of thinking.

Since I was teenager, my mother has never approved of my relationship with my boyfriend. "He's no good for you." She says it all the time. I think he's a good man. He is understanding and can help guide me in life. My boyfriend is bighearted person and her perception of him amazes me. But my mum always judges a man from his life's stability. Even though I know that she is just trying to watch out for me, our way of thinking is totally different.

My mother always demands that I, her only daughter, look pretty and look after my appearance. My mother wants me to take care of my hair and face as much as possible. My mother always wants me to maximize my looks, but I prefer to maximize my values. I would like to be able to heal and give happiness to people.

These differences make me very stressed. I don't like feeling that I can never make my mother happy. I often blame myself because I cannot make my own mother happy, no matter how hard I have tried. I love my mother dearly. I want to be the best in front of her and give the best for her, because I know that my mum loves me very much and wants the best for me. But still, even if we love each other, but we also hurt each other.

I have always believed that every situation happens for a reason. It is not just a coincidence that I "chose" to be born from her. To know the reasons behind these family conflicts, I tried to do my own past lives regression to better understand my relationship with my mother.

Q: What do you see?
A: I am in an open green field.

Q: Can you see yourself?
A: Yes. I am a teenager. I'm wearing a European outfit.

Q: What is your name?
A: Marichzka. Hmm, someone came up to me.

Q: Who is it?
A: A boy. He is blonde and has quiff. His name is Daniello. He is my boyfriend.

Q: Why he is there?
A: He just wants to see me. We were playing around, and he gave me flowers. I was very happy.

Q: After that, what you are doing?
A: I went home. When I got home, my mum shouted at me. (My previous mum is my mum in my current life.)

Q: Why she's shouting at you?

A: She disapproves of my relationship with Daniello. She said that he is not the right man for me because Daniello has nothing. I cried and ran to my room.

Q: What will you do?
A: Daniello knew that my mum didn't approve of our relationship. That's why he asked me to leave the house and live with him.

Q: Did you agree to do it?
A: Yes. Daniello asked me to wait at the warehouse. He came and took me. We went through the wood. It was really cold, and I was terrified. We are planning to get married and live in a house, far from where my mother lives.

Q: Did you make it?
A: We walked quite far. Daniello fell asleep because he was too tired. I could not sleep because I was terrified. Then, bunch of men came to capture us.

Q: Who were they?
A: They were my mother's bodyguards.

Q: What they have done to you both?
A: They took us back to my mother's house. She was very mad to both of us.

Q: What was his reaction?
A: Daniello said that he wants me to be happy. But, my mum kept yelling at him. He left and was broken hearted.

Q: Let's move forward in time in your life after that night. What happened?
A: After that night, I lived with my mother again.

Q: Now, we are moving forward to the most important moment of Marichzka's life. What do you see?
A: It was very late at night. Daniello was drunk and he wanted to get in the house. He was carrying a knife. He threatened my mum. She and I were terrified!

Q: What did Daniello do next?
A: He left and I never saw him again.

Q: Let's move forward a few years to see how your life is after Daniello left. What are you doing at this moment?
A: I decided to find work in town. I work in a delicatessen. Every Sunday, I go home to my mum's house. I feel like this is the only way to be far from her.

Q: Are there any interesting moments at this time?
A: My mum yelled at me and come to the shop. She forced me to go home because a neighbor told her that I felt happy to be free and far from her. She felt angry and offended.

Q: Have any other important things happened?
A: Yes. I know this guy—he is a customer in the shop. He is a very success businessman. We like each other.

Q: Did you tell him about your mother?
A: Yes. When my relationship with him was getting more serious, I told him about my mum's character.

Q: How did he react?
A: I was so relieved; he still wanted to marry me, even though he knew what my mother was like. He came to her house and asked her to marry me.

Q: What was her reaction?

A: My mother liked him and then approved of our marriage.

Q: You got married then?
A: Yes, we got married and live in town. Our marriage life is very happy.

Q: Now, we are moving forward to when the most important moment happens between you and your mother. What do you see?
A: My mother was ill. She felt that her time was almost over. She apologized for blaming me all the time and forcing me to do what she wanted. She acted like that because she was never happy with her life. My dad left her, and because of that, she always put the blame on me by forcing me to do things that she could not do in her own life. She was doing that because she wanted happiness for both of us. After we forgive each other, she passed away.

Q: Let's see your past life as Marichzka and relate it with your current life. Is there any relationship?
A: The same pattern happens again. My relationship with my mum is not very good because Marichzka's relationship with her mum was not good in the past.

Q: Why has it happened again?
A: Because I have not passed the lesson from it.

Q: What is the lesson that you missed when you lived as Marisczka in the past?
A: The lesson to keep quiet and not overreact when my anger appears.

Q: How you supposed to act towards your mum in your past life as Marichzka?

A: I should love her more. I have to discard all my bad thoughts of mum.

Q: So, how you should act towards your mum in your present life?
A: I should have stay quiet and listen when she is angry to me —it's because she's just worried about my life. I should love her more because I know that behind all the arguments, she loves me dearly and just wants to see me happy. Maybe that is the only way she knows how to express her feelings toward me.

Q: In your current life, how you remember and react when your mother is angry to you?
A: My mum just wants to be happy. I can choose to love my mother and makes her happy by listening to her all the time and by not reacting at all. In that way, she will be calm and her anger will be gone.

This regression made me notice the source of conflict between me and my mum. I can learn from the lesson about action and reaction (remember cause and effect law) that happens in every fight. When she is mad, I realize that is an action of anger—and every action that appears will disappear. My mother's action of anger will disappear sooner or later. But, if I react to her anger, then I will cause her to become angrier and this will cause a new reaction. If this continues, her angry cycles will be longer.

Now I try to be more patient when facing my mum's anger. Every time my mum is angry with me, I will not spontaneously react to it. I just observe her anger and then ask myself, "Is her anger caused by my mistakes or just by her emotions and her worries?" I become more patient and try to control myself. All of this was impossible without my past lives' regression—before I was able to see how my relationship with my mother in my past life influenced my life.

Most people's anger comes from their own worries. They just need people to listen so they can express their worries. By being a good listener to an angry person, we become a "therapist" who is able to heal anger. By realizing that every action of anger will gradually disappear by itself, then you can stay calm and not react when someone expresses their anger. Being quiet and calm is a wise way to deal with anger.

"Everything will be passed. Anger will be passed. Be quiet and do not react."

Chapter 3

Lesson from Thunderbolt's Life

"I found that by doing what's best for us—doing something for good purpose, it allows us to become a good child."

During my childhood, I was close to my father. I always felt that he was a great and highly skilled person. Whenever I had questions, he always had good answers. He has always been there to guide me. He bought me my first computer and has always been there for me.

He is very responsible father. He pays for every course I take and makes sure I have everything I need. He even cooks porridge for me when I am ill. He is a great father.

When I began my courses at the university, I took a few seminars and I started my first business. In the beginning, I often discussed things I learned in the seminars with my father. But as time passed, I sensed that my father was resistant to new ideas. He seemed to think that the knowledge I gained from my seminars was inapplicable in daily life and business.

He began telling me that my new business would not be successful and profitable. He did not think I would succeed in running the business. As a result of his lack of confidence, I began to have questions that he could not answer. When I was young, he had great answers to all of my questions, but he could not answer these. Ultimately, we stopped discussing things, because we discovered that we have very different ways of thinking.

These changes between us bother me all the time. Now, I didn't think that he is a great father and I used to admire him. My father thinks that I do not want to get close to him anymore. Even though we are more distant with each other today, he remains a very good father to me. My father always supports me, despite out differing opinions, and I still think that he always be there when I need him. In fact, he always reminds me to eat.

In my regression, I sought to learn from our situation and perhaps find a solution. What do I need to do to become a good child to my father, and how I can be close again with my father like we used to be when I was little? This regression led me into one of my past lives in which I lived with my father.

Q: What do you see?
A: I am standing on the hill with my granddad. The view is amazing. As far as my eye can see, greenery and hills spread.

Q: Are you male or female?
A: I am an Indian male.

Q: What is your name?
A: Thunderbolt

Q: I want you to see your surroundings to know what is happening in that time. What do you see?
A: I see bunch of Indian men riding their horses and approaching us. They are wind soldiers. Their duty is to guard our village from attack from other villages. My granddad is training me to become one of the soldiers.

Q: I want you to move few years forward to see an important moment in the life of Thunderbolt. How old are you now?
A: I am fifteen years old.

Q: Are there any differences in you now, compares to few years ago?
A: Yes. I grew up to be a good-looking, athletic man. I know that girls in my village adore me.

Q: What is the most important thing happening in your life now?
A: Our village is being terrorized by night riders. They paint their faces white with black painting. They challenge us.

Q: We will move forward to see what will happen next. What do you see?
A: My granddad passed away. Before he died, he left a message for me to guard our village. Then, I decided to lead the Wind Soldiers to meet the White Face troops.

Q: Are you declaring war?
A: No, they declare that they do not want war. They just asked us to share part of our food source because they lack of food. I agree.

Q: Now, we move forward into the moment when you, Thunderbolt, meet your father in your present life. Where are you now?
A: In a cave. I am taking my horse to drink.

Q: Can you find your father?
A: Yes. I see this chubby Indian. He is one of the members who have duties to collect food for our people. He says that he wants to be a wind soldier like me, but his body is too fat and he cannot stand pain. He is my father in my current life. (Note: my dad in my current life is also chubby.)

Q: We will move forward to the important moment between you and your father in Thunderbolt's life. What happened?
A: Our village is attacked by the White Face troops. They want to dominate us. Me and the fat Indian were sent to warn the next village.

Q: What was the warning?
A: We needed to warn our neighboring village about what was happening to our village. Our village has been tricked by the White Face troops.

Q: Why was the fat Indian sent to accompany you?
A: Because he is one of food supplier in our village. He was sent to guarantee my food supplies during my journey to the next village.

Q: Do you succeed?
A: Yes. After a long journey through underground caves, finally we reached the neighboring village. I was awarded and honored to stay in that village. I even married the head village's daughter.

Q: What is your biggest achievement in your life as Thunderbolt? What do you see?
A: I was elected to be a head villager, and I lead the village with principles and justice.

Q: What happened to that fat Indian guy?
A: My fat Indian friend died because of fever he suffered from a wound on his stomach. He says that if there is a chance, he is willing to accompany me again in my journey. He will be food provider for me like he used to be, and by journeying with me, he hopes to learn to be a Wind Soldier.

Q: Let's move forward to the last moment of your life as Thunderbolt. How you die?
A: I died old next to my wife and kids.

Q: Now, let's discuss about the relationship between Thunderbolt's life and your own relationship with your dad

in your current life. As Thunderbolt, what have you learned about when you live with that fat Indian?
A: They only play a small part in my life journey, and they do the best they can to guide and support me so that I can achieve my purpose. Like my life when I was Thunderbolt, the fat Indian guy has contributed as food supplier during my journey to the next village to fulfill my mission. Without him, I doubt I could have completed the journey.

Q: Are you learning from your past life as Thunderbolt?
A: Yes. I more fully appreciate that the Indian guy has done the best he can to help me complete the journey successfully.

Q: From the lesson, how you should you appreciate the role others play in helping you?
A: By doing the best I can and fulfilling my purpose with happiness. There is no better way to appreciate others and to be thankful for other people's contribution and guidance in my life. I need to do my best and achieve my purposes with happiness.

Q: Next, what is the relevant about your past life as Thunderbolt and your relationship with your father in your current life?
A: I chose to born as my father's daughter because I knew that he is going to be a great father to me. I knew he would be a father who would do his best to fulfill his family's needs. He will do everything so that I can focus to my purpose in life— just like that Indian guy who helped me by providing food.

Q: So, what lesson you can learn from your past life as Thunderbolt that can help in your relationship with your father in your current life?
A: I need to appreciate my father more. Even though I want

him to be perfect so that I can once again discuss things with him, I need to realize that he is already perfect because he gives me the best he can.

Q: What should you do to appreciate and thank your father for his contribution in your current life?
A: By doing my best and achieving my purpose with happiness.

Q: By doing your best and fulfilling your purpose with happiness, will you be a good daughter to your father?
A: Everyone is waiting for us to reach our success. They will give their best if we do our best. My father is constantly giving to me, while he is waiting and hoping that I will do the best for my life. When I do my best and can achieve my purpose with happiness, I will be the best daughter for him. My dad realized that he has already given the best for his daughter so that she can achieve the best for her life.

After this regression, I appreciated and respected my father more. Differing opinions between us become less significant when compared to the scope of his contribution in my life. This regression makes me see another side of our relationship. This regression makes me stand up and see wider, rather than just seeing and judging my father from a daughter's point of view.

I appreciate him more for the little ways he is attentive to me and for the guidance he gives me. Even if he just reminds me to drink lots of water to keep myself fit. With this new consciousness, I am able to recognize how remarkable my father's attention and his loving care is in my life. I could not see this before the regression.

This regression has helped me understand a daughter's devotion to her father. I always presumed that my biggest achievement in life would be when I became a dedicated child and, therefore, made my parents happy. This is what makes me keep asking the same questions: "How to be a dedicated child to my parents?" and "How to pay them back for their good deeds?" From this regression, I found that by doing my best—doing something for good purposes—I am a good child. Success as a child is not just about dedication to our parents but also dedication to our country and even the universe.

"Do the best to achieve good purposes. Then other people will give their best for those good purposes, because the good vibe will spread from heart to heart."

Chapter 4

Annette and the Birthmark

"Every thought, saying, and deed has that potential to hurt or heal other people."

I have big, brown, island-shaped birthmark on the right side of my back. My mother once told me that I have it because when she stepped on a brown bag when she was carrying me. She says that in her family it is a bad thing to step on brown bag when you are pregnant and that doing so will cause the baby to have brown birthmarks.

Despite the birthmark, she tells me that I should be grateful—at least it is not on my face.

I have visited dermatologists to try to have the birthmark removed, but they tell me birthmarks cannot be removed and that I don't need to worry about it if it doesn't bother me. But I still wonder where it came from.

After I learn about hypnotherapy and past lives regression method, I realized that nothing happens coincidently; there is a cause and effect for everything. I knew there had to be reason behind my birthmark. I began with my curiosity and I conducted my own self regression to find the answer.

The result of my journey was incredible! I found the cause of my brown birthmark.

Q: What do you see?
A: I see young men dragging away a couple of young girls who are crying and screaming! The men ignore their cries.

Q: What you are doing?
A: I am standing near the wall and watching.

Q: Why has your body become tense?
A: I know I will share that fate! My body has frozen up because I am frightened.

Q: Okay, forget this moment. This moment hass already passed and you will be fine. I want you to be calm and we can continue this regression.
A: Okay.

Q: Do you know your name?
A: My name is Annette.

Q: Where were you born?
A: Europe. It looks like Holland, but I am not sure.

Q: Do you know what year it is?
A: Vaguely…maybe 1100.

Q: What are you wearing?
A: I am wearing a knee-high, light-colored dress with a big skirt. It is not like what wealthy people wear. It is like a servant outfit.

Q: What do you do daily?
A: I work as a servant in a tavern.

Q: Can you describe the tavern?
A: It was built from wood. The floor is also wooden floor. All tables and chairs are made from wood. In the middle of the tavern there are few blocks of wood to support the roof.

Q: How old are you?
A: About 18 years old.

Q: Can you describe yourself?
A: My body is very thin. My skin is very light and smooth. I am very gentle and shy. My other maid friends and my boss are always mocking me. They say, I am more like a princess than a maid. Because of my gentle behavior, I am not like other maids who work very fast.

Q: Who visits the tavern?
A: Mostly men. They come to that place to drink and stay over if they are travelers.

Q: Now we are moving forward a couple of years to see important moments in your life as a maid. How old are you?
A: Now I am 20 years old.

Q: Are you still working as a maid in that tavern?
A: Yes. I am still working as a maid in the same tavern.

Q: What are you doing?
A: I am cleaning a table. I see a big man enter the shop. His face is rough and very unpleasant. His hair is shoulder length and it hang loosely. A few other men follow him.

Q: What is he doing?
A: He enters the shop then speaks to my boss.

Q: What has it got to do with you?
A: In between the conversations, they are pointing at me.

Q: Why has your body become so tense?
A: My time has come...I am very frightened! I remembered my friends' faces when they were crying and screaming two years ago.

Q: Please calm yourself. This moment already passed, and you are all right now. What do you mean by your time has come?

A: When the time has come, servants in this shop will be sold as prostitutes in a brothel house that belongs to that big guy. We all know that we will be sold to become prostitutes and that we will be treated as slaves. The prostitutes are kept in the brothel, and we have to serve men who want company, without resting. To satisfy them, often we have to be chained or tortured. We cannot leave the brothel. If someone manages to escape and then is caught again, she is tortured more than prisoners.

Q: Now, what is happening to you?

A: They take me to the brothel house. I am in a room. I try to fight them. I bite, I kick, I scream, and I do anything I can to make them release me. At that point, the big guy becomes mad and nuts because of my attitude. He orders his people to push me hard so that I fall downward on the floor. My arms and feet are tied. He roughly tears my clothes from my back. Then he talks about how smooth and light skinned my back is. He says that I should be punished very nastily! I am so terrified! I have no idea what he is going to do to me.

Q: Then, what happen next? I want you to see this moment only as an observer. You will not feel the pain because the moment is already passed.

A: That man orders his people to heat the charcoal iron in the fireplace. I see that man rubbing that hot iron over and over again against my back. That hot iron burns my skin! I feel that my skin was burnt and sore! I am screaming and shouting; it is so painful. A few men tied my arms and feet strongly, and then I passed out from the pain.

Q: Let's move forward couple of moments to see what happen next. What is happening now?
A: When I wake up, I find myself in a bed. My back is very sore, and I have very high fever. It is because of the wound on my back. I can feel the infected wound from my back. I am so thirsty. On the right side table, there is a glass of water, but I cannot reach it. My body is too weak and too painful to move. When it is time to eat, someone will throw the food tray through my room's door, but I cannot reach it or walk over to pick it up.

Q: Can you heal the wound on your back?
A: One day, I cannot eat and drink for days; I feel extraordinary pain on my back. It's like some one has torn my whole body apart. I clench my palm to deal with the pain until I cannot feel the pain anymore.

Q: What happened to you?
A: I am on top of my body. I can see my own body down there with the rotten wound on my back. I died.The suffering that Annette endured through in her life as a maid must have causes. I do a self regression to see why she accepts this incredible torture that causes her die so miserably. This is my regression result from Annette's previous life.

Q: Now, we are going to enter the previous life to see the cause of your torture and miserable death. That wound is your birthmark on your right side of your back. What do you see?
A: I was brown-skinned Indian man. I was wearing an Indian outfit and my chest was bare.

Q: Can you tell me what your daily life is like?
A: I live with other Indians from another tribe. There are not

many in our tribe. We move from one place to another. When it is time to move, our head villager will announce it. He knows the right time to move based on the movement of the stars.

Q: What crucial moment do you see from that time?
A: Recently our tribe has begun to feel unsafe because we lost couple of our animals—they were stolen by someone from another tribe. One afternoon, when I was watching the woods, I spied a man trying to steal animal. I chased after him until I got into the wood, but he was running too fast and I lost track of him.

Q: Now, let's see the crucial moment that caused you to be tortured and to die as Annette, and that resulted in the birthmark that you have now. Tell me, what do you see?
A: That night, I have a feeling that someone will try to steal our animal again. I sit next to the fire to keep an eye on the animals. When it's getting very late and most people are asleep, I hear sounds from bushes behind me. I come near it and capture a guy. I tied his arms and put him on the ground. I ask him questions, but he is mute! He only mumbles, and I do not understand what he is saying. There are a bunch of guards on duty that night. I tell them that I captured this man because he was hiding in the bushes behind my tent.

Q: What happens next?
A: They take the man and tie him to our sacrifice pole. They say that he's gone mute because our ancestors put a curse in his throat. To be able to make him speak, he has to feel great pain; when he can scream loudly, they say, the curse will vanish from his throat. Because I was the one who captured him, his soul was mine. I was the one who should torture him.

Q: Do you do it?
A: I am very frightened because I have never tortured anyone before. They give me a flaming wood stick and tell me to stab him with it. I am hesitant, but then finally, I stab the stick into his right back. I do it several times so that he can finally scream and talk.

Q: Can he talk then?
A: No! He faints because of the pain he suffered.

Q: Then, what did you do to that man?
A: They tell me to keep an eye on him, but I fall asleep. Before I fall asleep, I see that the mute man is still fainted and tied to the pole. When I wake up, it is morning and I notice that the guard has taken the guy off the pole. The guard tells me that someone noticed the guy stealing an animal and he needs to be punished for what he has done.

Q: What kind of punishment will he receive?
A: He will be hung on the pole, facing the sun so that the God of Sun will punish him and burn him.

Q: How long he will be hung?
A: A couple of days. Our head villager orders us to release him because his punishing time has finished.

Q: What he did he do after he was released from the pole? Did you see him?
A: I see him being released from the pole and can see his burnt, swollen, and red wound. He stares at me with eyes full of hate. It is as if I can feel his hate. He runs into the woods, and I never see him again.

Q: Now, we will review your past lives. What have you learn from these two past lives?
A: Every action, thought, and deeds that I chose will take form in a new life. The actions I chose—to torture that mute Indian guy by burning his back with flaming wood—has caused me to be born in my life as Annette in Holland. In my life as Annette, I died because of the burnt wound on my right back that I suffered from the torture.

Q: Was there any better way you could help dealt with the Indian man?
A: Yes. I was the one who captured him, his soul was mine. Because his soul was mine, I could have released him.

Q: Why do you think you should have released that guy?
A: Because I did not see him steal; I only accused him of stealing.

Q: What have you learned about if you had released that Indian man?
A: In every situation there are always free choices of action, thinking, and talk. Therefore, please choose ways to think, speak, and act that will make us and others happy.Choose right way to think, speak, and action that can give happiness to us and others. Then it is our choice to be happy.

Q: Is your deed to that mute Indian guy has effected your live as Annette that really sad? But why, in your current life, do you still have birthmark on your right back?
A: Someone's hatred takes a very long time to vanish. The Indian man's hate for me was so deep, because of all I did to him, that it has leave hatred in his heart. Therefore, the hate is still there, and I carry it into my current life as my birthmark on my right back.

***Q: What experience have you learn from your past life as an
Indian that has relevance in your current life?***
A: I can choose my own thoughts, words, and my deeds to hurt
someone else, but in the end, it will get back to me. Or, I can
choose to be a healer for someone else's heart ache through my
thoughts, my words, and my deeds.

The regression result from my past lives as an Indian
man and as Annette answered my questions about the origins
of my birthmark. Those stories also inspired an extraordinary
awareness within me.

Our past words, thoughts, and deeds have extraordinary
impacts. Every word, action, and thought has power to hurt or
heal other people. Those things we have done, both good and
bad, will also reappear in our current or future life.

The good news is that in every situation we face, we
have the option to think, speak, or act. We can always choose
our thoughts, words, and actions so that we can make ourselves
and other people happy.

Even though I know that it is really difficult to
implement a policy of goodness because it is really hard to
control what we say, do, or think, life always gives us an
opportunity to choose. We get to decide whether to make us
and other people happy or sad.

*"Our words, actions, and thoughts can heal other people and
ourselves. Are you willing to do it?"*

Chapter 5

Supportive Friendships

Friendships are come and go unexpectedly. I have had close friends since I was young, and we have always been together. I have often wondered if we will grow old together and live near to each other in the future too. But as time has passed and we have dealt with our own lives and futures, we have grown apart. We think very differently and don't feel comfortable with to each other anymore.

Frankly, our journey to fulfill our dreams is not easy; there are lots of obstacles and difficulties in the way. But during hard times, Gunawan and I found our closest friends: Alex and Joni, who accompany us on our life journey.

The four of us do not know why we feel very comfortable together. We feel that we have known each other for so long already.

Although we still have lots of disagreements, we always try to deal with disagreements quickly. We are trying to keep our friendship going. We have separated a few times, but then, we meet again and once again become best friends who understand each other. The four of us often fight and disagree with to each other, but there is always something that makes us forgive and forget. Whatever our disagreement, separation, or anger between us, we always find ways to get back together— even better than before.

The values of friendships are very important to me. And our friendships characteristics are very strongly bonded with one another. This makes me curious: why is our friendship so strong? If we are different, then why do we always get back together again? To answer those questions, I did a self regression to see our past lives.

Q: What do you see?
A: I see a couple of boys playing soccer.

Q: Can you see yourself?
A: Yes. I am a ten-year-old boy. I am thin with browned skin.

Q: Can you see Gunawan, Alex, and Joni in this moment?
A: Yes. I can see them. We are playing soccer bare chested.

Q: Which country are you in?
A: Thailand.

Q: Can you describe your surroundings?
A: Yes. Our village is small. Our land is reddish and the wooden houses are very simple. In the middle of our village field there is wooden water pipe to restrain the rain.

Q: Now, what do you see?
A: I can see Joni is sitting by himself. He is always a loner.

Q: Why is that so?
A: Because his parents are fighting all the time. His father is always angry, and when he is angry, he threats Joni's mum with a blade.

Q: Now, we will move forward to crucial moment for four of you. How old are you now?
A: Twelve years old.

Q: What do you see?
A: We are biking around the village.

Q: Where were you going and why?
A: We want to see a friend who will be pronounced as a monk. We went to a place in the wood. There is a small house with an altar.

Q: Let's move forward to when four of you are old to know your jobs. What are your occupations?
A: Gunawan and I continue our education to work for the government. Joni is a tailor. Alex is a merchant.

Q: Is there any crucial moment that time?
A: Yes. Joni was very depressed and his business was almost bankrupt. Me, Gunawan, and Alex donate to help his business again. Our only hope is that he will heal from his depression.

Q: Is it working?
A: No. It turned out that money is not the solution. Joni will always be depressed because all the problems he has in his life. It is like he will never be happy. (In his present life, every time he has a problem, he becomes introverted and goes off alone. He becomes sad and depressed.)

Q: So, have you find a way to help him?
A: Friendships. By being there as his friends and accompanying him during his hard times, we can help Joni feel comfortable and calm because he knows that his friends will always be around to help him. We will encourage him to deal with his problems. He needs his three closest friends to be a strong and happy person.When I travel to that past life, I enter another past life. I entered different life moment. I see myself, Gunawan, Joni, and Alex at the beach. We are making a fish net together. The four of us were very happy and cohesive.

Q: Which country are you in?
A: Thailand, in is a fisherman village.

Q: Is there any crucial moment in that time?
A: Yes. Joni was appointed as the fish supplier in our village. Fishes captured from our fishing activities were collected and kept in the warehouse. Joni was responsible for managing it and for finding buyers.

Q: You look nervous. What bothers you?
A: Yes. We already advised him several times to be careful. His is not an easy job and it relates to the whole village's interests. But he ignores our advice and says he knows what he's doing.

Q: What has Joni done?
A: He sells all the fish to a buyer. The buyer promises to pay on receipt of the last shipment. But it has been days, and there is no news from him.

Q: Did he already take all the fish from the village?
A: Almost. There are just few left over before the last shipment.

Q: So, how's Joni now?
A: Joni is frightened and depressed. A villager calls us. He asked us to go to his house immediately.

Q: What happen?
A: When we arrive at his house, we see Joni on his bed. He hardly breathes. He just took poisons. He says that if there any chance of him living again, he wants us to warn him about not doing stupid things. Then, he dies.

Q: What do the three of you do after Joni's death?
A: We work together to collect money to buy a boat. Then we always work together to catch fishes and share them evenly.

Q: What is your purpose in being reborn again?
A: To be best friends, so that we can support each other in our present lives. It is not an easy thing to deal with difficulties and problems in this life. Friendships are a crucial thing, and we need them to support ourselves. The four of us chose to be born as friends again to make us stronger in this life, because we know that we have the best friends in the world.

From this self regression, I realized that it is very important for us to have the best friendships. A good friend will be willing to help and guide us, and will let us know our mistakes. They can give us advice and direction and help forbid us from doing bad things. It is a treasure to have best friends in this world.

A good friend will offer his guidance to help his troubled friend. A true friend will be willing to accompany us and give us strength and inspiration to pass all difficulties in life, because he knows that it is not easy to face it alone.

"Just by being there as his best friend, we already make that person stronger and tougher."

Chapter 6

My Murderer is My Best Friend

"This regression taught us to always give kindness, because of that, I will receive kindness in return."

In my previous chapter, I have mentioned that Gunawan and I have a best friend named Alex. We talk with him often, exchange ideas, plan our future together, inspire each other, and share many things that make us grow wiser. Our friendships really bond us, and we treasure our friendships very much.

However, our friendships did not occur by chance. We passed our trial stage, which was not an easy thing. There were lots of misperceptions and suspicions between us in the beginning. Alex thinks that Gunawan and I did not fully share our knowledge with him because Gunawan and I are bonded as partners and lovers in planning our future together.

Gunawan is a great dreamer and thinker. He makes plans for our dream to reach *financial freedom*. Alex thinks that we did not share our plan with him fully. We think that Alex comes to us only when he needs solutions to his problems. After he gets what he wants, he just leaves us.

There is something else that bothers me sometimes. I feel uncomfortable being around Alex without Gunawan. I feel awkward that I have to keep a distance from him. From the way I talk to him, I have clearly never felt comfortable with him. When Gunawan is around, I feel alright with Alex. Gunawan's presence makes me feel comfortable and protected all the time. One day, I told Alex how I feel about him and was surprised to find that he felt the same way too. How strange!

After our discussions, we decided to do self regression

into our past lives to know what had happened in the past and to understand why we were back together as best friends in our present lives.

Q: What do you see?
A: There are three six-year-old boys swimming on the beach.

Q: Can you recognize them?
A: Yes. They are me, Gunawan, and Alex.

Q: Now, what do you see?
A: There is a lady coming towards us. She is Alex's mum; she gets angry and slaps him. She is also very angry at us because we took him to the beach.

Q: Which country are you at now?
A: Thailand, at Pattaya beach.

Q: What is your name, Alex's name, and Gunawan's name in that life?
A: Is that important?

Q: Okay, if you don't feel is necessary. What year is it?
A: I am not quite sure…but maybe around 1900.

Q: Let's go back to when Alex's mum was mad. Why she was shouting at him?
A: Me and Gunawan go to his house and peep through his window. I see Alex was feeding his sick dad. She was mad because Alex had been playing too long and forgot to give lunch to his sick dad.

Q: Why couldn't his mum feed his dad?
A: Because she has to work as fisherman because his dad is ill

all the time.

Q: Now, let's fast forward to a time when you are a teenager. What do you see?
A: Me and Alex are knitting fish nets. Alex and I are fishermen.

Q: Where is Gunawan?
A: Gunawan lives in the temple. He is a soon-to-be monk and he lives there to study.

Q: Why did he want to become a monk?
A: He says that it is his choice. To be a monk, he becomes peaceful and wise. (In his current life, he always touches by simple things and cries easily every time he sees monks wearing Thai robes.)

Q: Let's move forward a couple of years to see a crucial moment in your life in Pattaya. What happening?
A: Gunawan came up to me when I was making fish net. He is already a monk.

Q: What for?
A: To ask me to be a monk like him. He often comes to me and tries to persuade me to become a monk.

Q: Do you agree with him?
A: Never! Even though I have always wanted to be a monk. But my life now is happy. Everyday I catch lots of fish; the villagers respect me because of that.

Q: Does Gunawan also ask Alex to be a monk?
A: Yes, but he ignores Gunawan. Alex says he has to catch lots of fishes for his family. Because of his father's illness, he

cannot work anymore. He wants to catch just as much fish as I do for his family.

Q: *Why does Gunawan ask you both to be a monk like him?*
A: Because he wants us to feel the peacefulness that he feels now and so that we can study and grow old together.

Q: *Now, let's move to the moment when that caused you to feel uncomfortable around Alex. What do you see?*
A: I am fighting with Alex.

Q: *Why?*
A: He is angry because I always catch more than him. He accuses me I of using magic to catch the fish, but I did not do anything! I just predict the right time to catch fish.

Q: *Why did he accuse you that?*
A: Because I go to the temple quite often.

Q: *Why you go there often?*
A: To see Gunawan. He has been my best friend since we were young. He is the only person I can talk to when I feel down. I go to the temple to seek his advice. His advice always calm me down.

Q: *Why not just tell the truth to Alex about it? Why not just tell him when the best time to catch fish is?*
A: Because he never asked me. He just accused me.

Q: *Why didn't you tell him without waiting for his question? Aren't you best friends?*
A: Because Alex never shares his catches with other fishermen. We always share our catches with others if they did not get any fish for the day. But he is a very introverted person. When he

catches lots of fish, he will hide them and take all of them home.

Q: Let's fast forward to see what happen after the fight. What do you see?
A: I am sitting alone on the beach. I am suddenly shocked and can feel pain in my back. I feel that I have been stabbed from behind.

Q: I want you to not to feel the pain. This moment already passed. Who stabbed you?
A: (I turn my head slightly) Alex killed me.

Q: Are you dead?
A: I am floating on top of my own body. I see Alex crying next to my body. Alex feels sorry about killing me, because he realizes that it won't make him catch more fish. He just got carried away and killed me. Instead of asking and learning from me how to get more fish. But, I don't hate him.

Q: Why are you crying?
A: I feel sad because I have to leave Gunawan. After my soul left my body, I went to visit Gunawan in the temple. I saw him meditating. I feel sad because I have to say goodbye to him. I wish I had listened to his advice to become a monk, maybe now I would be meditating and not saying goodbye this soon. If I have second chance, I will listen and do everything he says.

Q: What can you do in this life to avoid that incident?
A: I was supposed to tell Alex how to catch fish properly and when is the right time to do it, without being concerned about if he will give some of the fish to locals or keeps them all himself.

Q: Would it be better if you had just become a monk with Gunawan?
A: Yes, I should have listened to him and acted as his best friend. And if I become a monk, I would be a wiser person. I could be very smart person like Gunawan in his present life. I failed to learn that lesson in Pattaya.

Q: So, what should Alex have done to avoid killing?
A: He should have asked me how to catch fishes properly instead of accusing me without proof that I was using magic.

Q: What is the relationship between your past life and your present life?
A: It seems that there is repetition pattern. In my current life, Alex thinks that I do not want to share my knowledge and plans with him. It is similar to my past life when he thought that I used magic to get more fish. I don't share my knowledge because I feel that he only comes to me when he needs solution to his problem. Then, after he gets what he wants, he just leaves me.

Q: After reviewing your past live back in Pattaya, do you know what you are supposed to do?
A: Yes. I will give myself as a best friend for Alex so that Alex will become my best friend.

After this self regression and seeing our past lives in Pattaya, Thailand, the three of us speak heart to heart. Gunawan and I try to give and share with Alex and get rid of our negative perceptions about him. We believe that by giving sincerely, we will receive sincerity in return and Alex's negative perception of us and his suspicions toward us will vanish. We will be open about things and discuss them together to avoid misperceptions and negative interpretation. Now, that uncomfortable feeling has gone. I can talk to him without feeling awkward. Our friendships are stronger and we will continue to learn how to be good friends to each other.

This regression taught me that if I always give goodness, then I will receive goodness. I've discovered that after I implement those kindnesses, miracles happen in my life. I feel like I am growing to be a happier person than I was. If you want goodness to happen in your life, then you should give goodness to someone else. Then, miracles will happen in your life.

"To give and to get"

Chapter 7

Lesson for Mirriam, the Slave

When I joined the Multi Level Marketing (MLM) business, I had lots of opportunities to attend seminars and seminars are the fastest way I know to learn something. My network marketing seminar opened my mind; I learned that the power of the mind is unlimited. Anything is possible if we just believe of what we do and have a strong commitment to do it.

While studying *network marketing*, I met a teacher, Agnes (not her real name), who shocked my reality. One afternoon, she invited me, Gunawan, and my other two friends to chat in a coffee shop. I can remember the moment that afternoon when she turned my "reality blind shield" into a big screen so that I could see everything clearly. Agnes told me that she once attended a big seminar that cost 75 million rupiah. It was a shocking thing for me to hear; at that time, 100 thousands rupiah was a lot of money to me.

Her story has influenced my view of reality, and I am thankful to her for that. She also told me stories about when she was backpacking in Tibet and the Himalayas. She explained that when she finally got to the top of the Himalaya's peak that there was a very thin layer of air. She said those 40 days of her back-packing journey were very interesting and entertaining. Her stories exposed me to a glimpse of life on the other side of the coin.

Almost every member of my family has their own business or works in an office. My parents hardly ever have time to rest or have holidays because they have to open the shop daily. Listening to Agnes made me realize that there are times in our lives when we should spend time enjoying life and not focus exclusively on making money. I realized I was missing that way of life.

Agnes' strong influence on my current life made me wonder if I had met her in a past life. It was clearly not a coincidence that she was in my life now and had changed my way of thinking.

I decided to do a self regression to try to learn about Anges' role in my past life and why we were certain to meet again in this life.

Q: What do you see?
A: I am standing on top of the hill. I am staring at white painted houses with white fences in a green field.

Q: Are you a male or female? And what is your name?
A: I am a black girl. My name is Mirriam.

Q: How old are you?
A: In between six or seven years old.

Q: Where were you born? What year?
A: California, United States. The year is vague, but there is still slavery in the US.

Q: Do you have a family?
A: Yes. I have a father, a mother, and little brother. My dad works on a farm. He wears a hat all the time. My mum is chubby and likes to eat.

Q: Are they in your life now?
A: Just my mum. She is my auntie in my current life. She is also fat and likes to eat.

Q: We fast forward to the moment when you met Agnes, your current teacher in your life now. How old are you?
A: I am twelve years old.

Q: How do you meet her?
A: I am sold to work in a white family. My duty is to scrub wooden floors. I have a mistress, and she is my teacher now.

Q: Let's fast forward to the moment when we can see Mirriam's daily life. How old are you? What are you doing daily?
A: My job is not to scrub the floors anymore. My job is to serve food and clean my mistress' bed room. At night time, I read in my room. I like reading books.

Q: Where do you get those books?
A: I take the books from her—the ones that she never reads anymore.

Q: Who taught you to read? Normally black people cannot read, right?
A: I learned to read when I was young. Where I come from, there was a black lady who could read. She had been taught by her mistress and she taught the kids around my house to read. She taught me to read.

Q: We move forward to when your life as Mirriam interacts with your teacher. What happens?
A: I am in her bedroom, cleaning her room. She is on her bed. She asks me why I like to read.

Q: Is your husband is in your life now?
A: I don't know. I didn't know him in my current life.

Q: Are there any changes in your mistress' life now?
A: Yes. She is also married to a man with a high position in the local government. Her thoughts have major impact on his career.

Q: Now, let's move forward to your last moment as Mirriam. What happens?
A: I feel pain in my chest. I am in her kitchen. I go home and lie on my bed. My chest hurts so much.

Q: Did you die?
A: Yes. I left my body, and I can see my body down below. My husband and my children are crying beside my body.

Q: Now, we will review your past life as Mirriam. What have you learned?
A: I learned that the power of our mind is unlimited—far more so than our imperfect body and life.

I once heard this advice: "We were born with two ears and one mouth, so that we listen more than talk." I also hear it often in my few seminars and in books I read, but I never really seriously understood it.

After I became a hypnotherapist, I realized the power of that wise saying. It is true that most of us have a hard time being a good listener.

Almost every client I handle struggles to listen at the beginning of the session. They often have no hope that they can become a better person. Miracles happen though because, at the end of the session, they often feel so light—as if their problem has been solved. What have I done to make my clients to feel that way? Nothing! I just be a good listener to them and listen to whatever they choose to share with me.

Can we heal others just by being a good listener? I learn a lot by listening to their life stories. I learn that every problem carries a lesson. These problems occur so that we can take lessons from them and become wiser people, mentally and spiritually.

It is very hard for us to be good listeners, but when we truly listen—for example, in conversation with a good mentor, we are easy to advise. With that attitude, we also open ourselves and prepare to learn from another person's experience. And every time we learn and train to become a good listener, we can broaden our mind's reality and become wiser.

"Our mind reality will not be open by itself. It needs someone or a media to open it."

Chapter 8

My Soul Mate and Imaginative Prince

This time, I would like to share a story about my lover and my past life that we have been through together. Gunawan is a dreamer and a great planner. He has great dreams that open my reality to how much I can do for this country, and even for the world, if have the courage to be a dreamer. That is why I call him my Imaginative Prince.

I met him in our university organization. When I saw him for the first time, I felt like I had known him long ago. Then, we became very close when we worked together on the social event. Even if we grew very close quickly, our relationship was not easy. My parents disapproved my relationship with him.

They forced me to be separated from him. But our relationship was strong, and those barriers helped make us even stronger. We have survived and are even more committed to each other and solid as a couple than ever.

I admit that we often fight and argue about our different perceptions and characteristics, but then, those differences encourage us to understand each other. If one of us attends a seminar, the other one has to follow. We both believe that seminars can broaden our reality. We also believe that seminars are the right media to absorb new things in this hectic world.

I read most books that he reads, and vice versa. We often discuss the books we read, so that we can grow in knowledge and understanding together. Our hope is that we can be partners that can complete and support each other.

We have the same dream—to achieve financial freedom by a certain time; if we can be free financially, then we can give more to other people. This far, we are solid couple in reaching the dream.

Gunawan is my teacher. and I am his happiness in life. I can always make him laugh, and he always makes me enthusiastic. We play and joke around, but we are also serious team partners in making decisions and implementing our plans. All things we do to fulfill our dreams.

However, as a past lives regression practitioner, I would like to see my past life with him. Why is he in my life now, being near me and completing me? Why does it seem that he is here specially to be my guide, teacher, partner, and lover? Is he really my soul mate?

Q: Do you see yourself?
A: Yes. I am a little girl wearing red dress.

Q: What is your name?
A: Penelope.

Q: Which country are you in?
A: Spain.

Q: What year?
A: (After silence for a while…) around 1776.

Q: What are you doing?
A: I am outside the house with my mother. I am waving to a well-dressed man..,he is my friend. His name is Jacques.

Q: Are there any people in Penelope's life that you know now?
A: Yes. Jacques is Gunawan.

Q: Now, let's fast forward into a crucial moment between Penelope and Jacques. What do you see?
A: I am in this beautiful bedroom. I am married to Jacques. The bed is made from beautifully carved wood with white veils.

Q: Can you tell me what his job is at that moment?
A: Jacques sells local antiques and furniture to the international market. His business is expanding rapidly.

Q: So, what is your job?
A: My role is to give him lots of love.

Q: What do you mean?
A: I want to become a good wife for him by loving him dearly.

Q: We fast forward in few years time to see another crucial moment between Penelope and Jacques. What happened?
A: I just gave birth to a baby boy. Jacques is very happy that I gave him a son to continue his business. We are very happy with his birth.

Q: Now, let's see what your biggest achievement is when you are Penelope. What do you see?
A: Jacques and I have always been happy together. That is my biggest achievement, because we love each other sincerely.

Q: What can you and Gunawan learn from your past lives as Penelope and Jacques?
A: In our past lives as Penelope and Jacques, we learn that we have to continue to loving each other sincerely, and we also learn about loyalty. Jacques and Penelope's life was very beautiful, and it fills me with happiness. However, I would like to learn more. I do another self regression to see my other past life with Gunawan.

Q: Now, we will see your other past live when you and Gunawan love each other. Can you see yourself?
A: Yes. I am a ten-year-old girl. I am wearing a polka dot skirt, and I have blonde hair.

Q: What is your name?
A: Annette.

Q: What country are you in and what is the year?
A: America and it is around 1930.

Q: What are you doing?
A: I am enjoying the view. It's like I am in a spaceship, like a Star Trek movie. (Laughing). I am imagining Miss Jackson's explanation in front of the classroom. Miss Jackson is my teacher. She teaches us about outer space.

Q: Now, I would like to fast forward to the moment when you and Gunawan meet in Annette's life. What do you see?
A: I am in the middle of a prom night. Now, I am a beautiful young girl. I am sitting alone, and my other friends are dancing.

Q: Why aren't you dancing like them?
A: I have girl friends like other teenagers normally, but they just ordinary friends. I prefer to be alone, so that I can observe and learn.

Q: Is Gunawan there too?
A: A boy came up and sat next to me. He introduces himself; his name is Gandhi. He is mixed Indian American. Yes, I know him. Gandhi is Gunawan in my current life.

Q: What are you doing?
A: We are chatting, and I feel safe being with him.

Q: What are you talking about?
A: I ask him about India. Gandhi tells me about reincarnation and Karmic law. I feel like those concepts are suitable with my way of thinking and can answer questions that appear in my mind when I observe others.

Q: After graduating from your junior school, what do you do?
A: We continue our educations. Gandhi goes to financial school ,and I continue my study as a nurse.

Q: Why does he choose that subject?
A: Because he wants to continue his father's business.

Q: What kind of business?
A: His father owns a fabric and perfume business in India, and he wants to market them in America and Europe. Gandhi wants to expand the business.

Q: So, why do you choose to be a nurse?
A: I choose to be a nurse because that's normally what a girl chooses to be. I like that subject.

Q: Are you and Gandhi still having a relationship?
A: Yes. We continue to have a relationship. Even if we are apart, we were still in the same town.

Q: Is your relationship going all right?
A: Actually, my dad does not approve of my relationship with Gandhi because he is not a Native American. But because his father is a well known business man, eventually my dad agrees

to our relationship.

Q: We fast forward to the moment after you have finished college. What happens?
A: I marry Gandhi, and his business expands. I work as a nurse because I enjoy it.

Q: We move forward into another crucial moment between you and Gandhi. What happens?
A: Gandhi heard there is a teacher who has taught an unusual concept. He asks me to attend the seminar, and he seems to admire that concept.

Q: What are you doing next?
A: Gandhi decides we should take evening school together. Gandhi thinks that we should grow together. That is why he wants me to join him in evening school.

Q: What is evening school?
A: It is a school implemented by teachers. We do not earn degrees in this school, but knowledge is more important than a degree.

Q: Does your evening school contribute positively to your life?
A: Yes. Gandhi has implement the leadership concepts and other things taught by the school for his business. As a result, his business is expanding. Gandhi becomes a great leader for his company. I also implement the leadership concept into my subject, and as a result, my patients become happier and I become more dedicated to my profession.

Q: What have you learned from these past lives?
A: We continue to learn and grow together.

Q: From both of your past lives with Gunawan, do you know if he is your soul mate?
A: Yes. A soul mate is someone who can encourages you to dream to be a better person. Gunawan always opens my reality to have the courage to dream, and he guides me to always learn and grow together. Yes, he is my soul mate.

Q: So, what lesson have you learned for your current life?
A: Our lesson for our current life is giving each other. By giving to each other, it can lead to something bigger—to giving as much as we can to others.

Q: What does that mean?
A: It means that both of us have missions. And we can achieve that mission if we keep on giving sincerely and dearly.

Q: What is your mission now?
A: My mission is to be a healer. I would like to take lots of people to remarkable spiritual journeys in their own minds. I would like to connect them with their best achievement in their lives. Gunawan will be my imaginative prince. He will be responsible and make plans for me to achieve my mission. And after that, I will connect him to his highest strategy to find his next mission.

Q: What do you mean by saying that you can achieve that mission if we can give to each other sincerely and dearly?
A: I can achieve my mission if Gunawan guides me to be a healer. It means that Gunawan will give himself to me to be my imaginative prince. After I become a healer, I will connect him with his highest strategy. I will take him to search and accompany him in the next mission, to become an imaginative prince for lots of people. Together, we will be a healer and an imaginative prince for lots of people.

From this regression, I have come to understand that how important it is for every couple to know their mission together and that it is going to be a key or love binder for their commitment. Each of them will realize that they need to be together to be able to finish their mission. The couple will be solid and inseparable, if they realize that they are nothing if they are alone. This awareness will be a strong guidance in their love and commitment.

This is my new understanding of my soul mate. Really, love and commitment become our guide in continuing to love each other and be loyal, because it is not an easy thing to stay loyal and guard our hearts.Every couple needs to strive to understand their mission together. By knowing it, they can choose to love each other for a higher purpose and to finish this spiritual journey together.

"A soul mate is someone who can encourage us to dream to be a better person."

Chapter 9

Past Life Karma and Fear

"Life is a battle field because it presents many difficulties, barricades, and temptations."

What would happen if we were faced with our biggest fear? What would you do if your soul and life was at risk? Would you deal with it and just follow your heart, or step back to save our own life?

These questions have been in my mind ever since Gunawan told me that his uncle had been recently infected by HIV and that he was coming to live with Gunawan. His uncle had been very sick and doctors had been unable to diagnoses the problem. One doctor ultimately recommended he take an HIV test, and the result came back positive.

Gunawan's uncle is in pretty sad condition; he has lost a lot of weight, and his skin hangs on him like loose clothes. He has gone blind in both eyes and he is losing his memory. After seeing his uncle's condition, Gunawan was touched and decide to take him to his house. I worry because HIV/AIDS is not an ordinary disease, it's the scariest disease in the world!

Gunawan tells me that his heart led me to make that decision. He has to carry his uncle to help him. He realized that bring his uncle to his home and taking care of him there was the best way to do it. As his closest friend and lover, of course, I understand this.

However, when you live with a person who has HIV/AIDS, there is an increased risk of contagion. We have tried to gather as much information as possible about contagion. The Internet is the easiest and fastest way to gain knowledge about this contagious disease. We know it spreads through sexual fluids and blood contact. We can get infected if this liquid gets in into our body system. HIV/AIDS infections occur primarily through a sexual relationship with infected individual, by exchanging needles, through blood transfusions that carry HIV/AIDS viruses, and by bodily fluid contact with an open wound. But if we only share eating equipment and contact with their sweat, tears, saliva, or urine, there is no possibility that we will get infected. That's why there is no need to be worry about shaking hands, touching, or even hugging them.

But fear is irrational. We can study this disease and understand how it infects, but we are still afraid of it. Gunawan and I listen to our deepest hearts and try to face that fear. We accept and take care of his uncle sincerely. We would like to give him the best present in his life by accepting and caring for him dearly.

Our acceptance and action was supported by my past life regression together with Gunawan and his uncle.

Q: What do you see?
A: I see a homeless neighborhood; the children are dirty and filthy. The neighborhood is dark and stinks in the afternoon.

Q: Can you see yourself?
A: Yes, I am a Dutch lady.

Q: What are you doing in that filthy area?
A: Every day, I pass that area. I always watch them, I even stop by and get off my car to see them.

Q: Which country are you in?
A: Indonesia. A lot of Dutch people live here. We dominate their government.

Q: Was that when the Dutch colonized Indonesia?
A: Yes, you are right.

Q: What is your name? How old are you?
A: They call me Esmeralda, I am 18 years old. I am the daughter of a Dutch official.

Q: Is there someone you know from the past when you were Esmeralda?
A: Yes. In that neighborhood, there is a leader. He orders his people to work. He is in charge and admired by others. He is my boyfriend's uncle in my present life who got infected by HIV/AIDS. Then, there is a guy my age, that man's nephew. He is different from other homeless people. He is quiet and I feel that he is better than the others. He is not supposed to be there; he is now my lover in my present life.

Q: Do you have contact with him?
A: Yes. I brought him home to be my gardener.

Q: Can you describe your house?
A: My house is pretty big, and the garden is broad. The wall is white; the floor is light brown with a dark brown pattern. In the front yard, we have a flower garden, and in the back yard, there are rooms for the house maids.

Q: Now, we will find out what caused your boy friend's uncle got HIV/ AIDS infected. What was the caused?
A: That young man who was my gardener says that his uncle often sleeps with maids that he thinks are pretty. And no one dare to stop him; many of them got pregnant. He also says, his uncle asks him if he wants to choose a girl to sleep with.

Q: Does he do it?
A: No. It's against his principles.

Q: What principles?
A: I don't know. He is very honest, a hard worker and a quiet person.

Q: To see your relationship now with him, is there any special relationship between Esmeralda and the gardener?
A: I like him and he likes me, although he never actually said that to me. But I was engaged to a young Dutch officer. We have been matched since we were little.

Q: We fast forward to few years ahead to see the connection between you, your boyfriend and his uncle in Esmeralda's life. What do you see?
A: My gardener came to the house with his uncle. My gardener asked my permission to take his uncle to live with him. He looks old and ill.

Q: Were they permitted?
A: Yes. I feel sorry for him.

Q: Can you move forward to a crucial moment for the three of you in Esmeralda's life?
A: Yes. There are a lot of Indonesian soldiers attacking Dutch colonial houses. They enter my house and there are many of them.

Q: Please calm yourself. This moment already passed. Now, I want you to explain it to me calmly.
A: My gardener takes me to hide in his house. Those people search every room in our house.

Q: Did they harm your family?
A: No. They are out of town. It is just me and the maids.

Q: Did they find you?
A: No. When they search my maids' house, my gardener and his uncle make sure that there are no Dutch people in the house. They save my life.

Q: After that, what did you do?
A: I marry my fiancé.

Q: Did you meet the gardener and his uncle after you got married?
A: Never.

Q: Do you still love your gardener?
A: Yes. I love him my whole life.

Q: What lesson do you take from Esmeralda's life?
A: I should have listened to my heart. I should have lived in Indonesia and married my gardener, but I chose to life my live comfortably and moved back to Holland.

Q: Is there any relationship between the lesson and your life now?
A: Yes. In my past life as Esmeralda, I couldn't pass my lesson, which is to listen my own heart. Now, I experience it again. I have to deal with a situation where I have to choose between my heart's intuitions by accepting my boyfriend's uncle with HIV/ AIDS or to step back to save my life.

Q: Why, in your life now, do you feel a very strong encouragement to help his uncle?
A: In his past life, the gardener's uncle had taken care of him

since he was little; his uncle treated him like his own son. That is why, in his current life, my boyfriend feels a very strong wish to help his uncle. He thinks it's payback time.

Q: So, what is your concern?
A: In my past life as Esmeralda, they saved my life. This is a repetition cycle. As Esmeralda, I never listened to my intuition because I chose to live comfortably. Now, the cycle is repeating again.

Q: Is in your current life, have you listened to your intuition?
A: Yes. I have listened to my heart by accepting his uncle. I love him just like my own family, and I interact with him without fear. This time, my encouragement to help him is stronger than my fear to keep my life safe.

Q: So, what has happened to your boyfriend's uncle's life is also a repetition cycle?
A: Yes. In the past, his uncle couldn't control his desire and slept with homeless women. Now, he also cannot control his desire and was infected by the HIV/AIDS viruses because of the same act.

Q: Now, what can he do to reduce his suffering?
A: What can he do now? He's not able to pass this obstacle in his present life or in his past life. He still has to deal with it in his future life.

Q: Is there any way for him to deal with this repetition cycle?
A: Perhaps in the future, he can choose to face it and win the battle. But because he did not know it, he makes the same mistakes again and again.

This regression is not just about getting rid of our

paranoia, but also it gives us a lesson about the life cycle. How wonderful it would be if everyone could see their own past lives. Then they would be able to see their mistakes and avoid repeating them again and again. They can choose to deal with itand break that repetitious cycle.

Many temptations and difficulties come and go in our life and we don't always have options. Whatever our efforts, or no matter how hard we try, difficulties and temptations still come into our life. But that is life.

Life temptations always get in through our wide-open senses, without any shield or barricade. Our eyes easily see beautiful and dazzling things; our ears can hear things—good or bad. Our nose always smells perfumery, and our body always feels touching sensation. All those things that absorb our senses force us to deal with problems. If our senses accept all things that get in, then what can protect us from life's temptations. Just our self control.

Life is a battle field that can present difficulties, problems, and temptations. Why they do they exist? They exist so that we can practice to self perfection and increase our level of consciousness. If we can do that, then we will be ready for the next life. If we can pass life's difficulties, temptations, and troubles, then we will better enter our next life. Who else will help us deal with those situations? Everyone must fight their own battle and use self-control and commitment to discipline to overcome those obstacles.

Whatever difficulties and temptations we have, no matter how hard they are, there is only one way to deal with it —self control. Face it and do it right.

"Everyone is facing their own battle. Don't be afraid and never give up! Just face it and do the right thing!"

Chapter 10

The Cause of My Auntie's Cancer

"If we cannot predict the unfortunate moments that caused by our mistakes in the past, then the only thing we can do is to do everything right all the time."

I was very close to my auntie. She was like my best friend. She was always giving me advice. She started her own business at a very young age. She did it with courage and hard work. She was an independent woman and always optimistic. I admired her and always listened to her advice.

My auntie said," In this life, we desire many things, but it doesn't come to us. So we have to fight for what we want in this life."

My auntie was a great woman. Although she was young, she had already achieved success. Tragically, in the end, my auntie passed away at the age of 32. She had stage four brain cancer.

Six months before she died, she spent her time in the hospital. She had two brain surgeries. Her blood and brain fluids were constantly flowing from her head. Her memory was weak, she had gone blind, and her body was half paralyzed. Even when she suffered badly, she wanted her family around to guide and take care of her. When she was alive, she was a devoted child and helped her family a lot. My auntie was a very loving person and acted as a guide to other people. She was a nice person and full of life, but she has to deal with the disease that eventually took her life.

She was a great and very devoted person, but her suffering made me wonder. Why did she die that way and at such a young age? I did a self regression to find out.

Q: What do you see?
A: Lots of trees. They are not too green or bushy.

Q: Do you see your body?
A: No.

Q: So, what were you?
A: Nothing. No shape. I am just consciousness.

Q: Now, we are moving forward when you were with your aunty in this life. What do you see?
A: There is a man; he is my auntie in my current life, and he was carrying a big fish. He takes it home and cuts it into pieces.

Q: Why did he carry that fish?
A: To make smoked fish and sell it in the market.

Q: Let's move forward to find out the cause of her brain cancer in her life now. What do you see?
A: I see a piece of brain on the plate.

Q: What brain?
A: A monkey brain.

Q: Why there was monkey brain there?
A: That young man likes to hunt. He hunts black monkeys. After he hunts them, he ties them and takes their brains.

Q: What for?
A: He eats some and sells the rest.

Q: Why did he eat and sell those brains?
A: He thinks that eating monkey brain makes him smarter.

That's why he eats them, and he sells those brains to get money. By doing that, he feels happy, because he presumes that by selling those monkey brains, he makes people become smarter.

Q: Is that the cause of your auntie's brain cancer now?
A: Yes, that's the way it is.

Q: So, what did you do then?
A: I am just an observer, and I observe that man's life.

Q: Why were you just an observer?
A: It is part of my learning process. I observe that man life so that I can learn from him. There are souls that are present in one moment of life just as an observer. These souls just act as observers; they just contribute as spectators, without feeling involved or influencing people's lives.

Q: So, what lessons have you learnt as an observer in that man's life?
A: To see how someone's misperception has caused him to do a bad deed, and how happy and satisfied he feels by doing that.

Q: Can you explain it?
A: His misperception was that by eating monkey brains will make him smarter. Then he killed monkeys happily, because of his wrong perception.

Q: Tell me how his bad deed affected his life now?
A: My auntie was a very nice person. She was a positive thinker, a hard worker, a diligent person, and she obeyed her parents. She helped her relatives sincerely. She was an auntie, a sister, and a good daughter who inspired everyone in every aspect. She was an extraordinary person, but it was too bad that

she had to die young in such a miserable way.

Q: What lesson you have learnt from your auntie's past life?
A: I learned that bad deeds in the past will cause bad things to happen in a future life.

Q: What lesson can you get from this regression?
A: Bad deeds in the past will follow you, just like a shadow follows its subject.

Our bad deeds will get back to us in the end. Those causes condition us to suffer from disasters, diseases, bankruptcy, poverty, and unfortunate situations in this life. No matter how hard we try to avoid them, bad deeds from the past will follow us. We never know what kind of bad deeds we have done in the past, and the causes that follow us will come to us at anytime.

If we cannot predict those bad lucks from bad deeds we have done in the past, the only thing we can do is to do good deeds as much as we can, so that we will have positive expectations in the future. Hopefully, those good deeds will be able to help us to deal with problems like disasters, diseases, bankruptcy, poverty, unfortunate situation, and other difficulties we are facing now.

"Causes of bad needs will follow you continuously like shadows that follow their subjects."

Chapter 11

Multiple Soul Mates

"Every soul mate that is present in our life now will contribute
a 25% chance of becoming our appropriate soul mate. But
still, 75% is the commitment that has to be placed in our life
now."

My relationship with Gunawan has been going on for years. We are always together. We are *best partners* and best friends. People who just know us can see that we love each other. Because we are so close, I cannot imagine loving another man as much as I love Gunawan. And he also thinks that way. That is why I feel that he is truly my soul mate.

Our harmonious relationships continue to flow, but there are moments when temptation appears. There was another love that once appeared between us, and we were tempted to be disloyal and to have an affair. I remember the afternoon when Gunawan and I were eating in a restaurant, and I told him that I was falling in love with another man.

"To be honest, that feelings appear just like that, when first time I talk to him", that's how I fight my feelings.

This other man and I meet each other quite often because he is my colleague. The feelings we have grow and we like each other. He phones me sometimes, and we like to discuss things together. The feelings just began to appear and grew to be a presence between us.

I intentionally told Gunawan about the feelings I had for this other guy, because inside my deepest heart, I didn't want to have feelings for this other man. I told Gunawan so that I could love him more fully without someone else between us!

Surprisingly, Gunawan had already realized it. The most shocking thing was that he was also in love with someone else.

"I can't control my feelings toward him. That feeling appears at first sight," he told me frankly.

He says that our commitment and loyalty were being tested. We decided to do nothing, and to let the feelings disappear on their own. We knew that something that could appear on its own could also disappear on its own. Those loving feelings happened spontaneously and were not invited, just like a cancer that appears suddenly inside a healthy body. We both felt hopeless toward those feelings.

I cried for days. My trust had been torn into small pieces. How was it possible that we could both fall in love with someone else when we knew that we were truly soul mates and we had a mission to accomplish together?

To cope with the situation, we needed to think clearly. We decided to hold hands so that we didn't get dragged away by this problem and become disloyal to each other. Then, I searched for enlightenment within my confusion and tried to find the solutions to these problems.

Q: What do you see?
A: A beautiful lake inside a cave.

Q: Do you see yourself?
A: Yes. I am a daughter. I am swimming in that cave.

Q: Is there someone else there with you who is also in your life now?
A: Yes. I am swimming with a guy. He is my boyfriend. We aree very happy and we love each other.

Q: Is he in your life now?
A: Yes, he is the guy that I like in my present life.

Q: Now, let's move to the crucial moment between you and the guy. What do you see?
A: In the crowd, there are many people on the street. There are lots of horse riders and carriages passing by.

Q: Are you still in the same life with the life that you have when you were swimming on the lake?
A: No. It is different life.

Q: What can you see with you and the guy in this life?
A: Yes, we are hugging each other. He is my boyfriend. In this life, we love each other and we are soul mates.

Q: What was your relationship with that guy in both of your past lives?
A: We are soul mates who love each other in these two past lives. We love each other and live together happily.

Q: Now, we will enter your past life to see your relationship with other guy. What do you see?
A: I am sitting on top of a hill and staring at the beautiful beach. Someone calls me Nouna.

Q: Who calls you?
A: Abram, my boyfriend. He is my boyfriend in my current life. We both go down the hill and play on the beach. I am very happy. Abram and I love each other.

Q: What did you do next?
A: We came to Paul, who was sitting on the beach. He looks sad. Paul is another man that I like in my current life.

Q: What does Paul do in this life?
A: Paul loves me too, but Abram and I have loved each other

since we were young. Paul is sad because we are getting married.

Q: Let's move to the crucial moment for the three of you. Where are you?
A: Abram and I are leaving a restaurant. We are happily married. Suddenly, Paul walks up to us and slaps Abram.

Q: Why did he hit Abram?
A: Paul says, it's because Abram won and has made his life miserable. Then after that, he leaves and I never see him again.

Q: What is your relationship with Abram and Paul in this life?
A: In this life, Abram was my soul mate. Paul loves me because he still has feelings from his past life. In the past, I was his soul mate.

Q: Now, we enter your other past life to see what happen between you, your lover, and the girl that he likes. What do you see?
A: Many sick people. They are vomiting and they look very weak. I can see dying people everywhere—inside houses and on the streets.

Q: Can you see yourself?
A: Yes. I am a nurse. I am wearing a Korean outfit.

Q: What happens in that moment?
A: There is a weird contagious disease attack our village. Most of the villagers are dying.

Q: We will move forward to the moment when you met your lover and that girl. Where are you?
A: I am in a room feed a dying old lady.

Q: Who is she?
A: She is a royal family member. That time, I was working as a nurse in her house. That old lady is the mother of the young prince.

Q: Do you know them now?
A: Just the prince—he is my current boyfriend.

Q: What happens next?
A: The lady died, and then I feel the same symptoms, I feel sick and begin to vomit.

Q: We fast forward to see what happen to you next. What are you doing now?
A: I am lying on my bed. Now I live in that house and they take care of me as a way to thank me for taking care of his mother.

Q: What happen now?
A: The young prince's wife also got infected. She is very weak. He loves her so much; he takes care of her every day. I see them from behind my door. I really admire his love for his wife.

Q: Can you recognize the young wife in your life now?
A: Yes. She is the girl that my boyfriend likes now.

Q: What happen to you next?
A: His wife finally passes away. The young prince is really sad because he has lost his beloved wife. I leave the house because

I cannot stand to witness his sadness. Secretly, I love him deeply.

Q: Where did you go and what happens to your life next?
A: I lived in the wood until I died.

Q: What is the relationship between the young royal with his wife in your life now?
A: They are soul mates in this life.

Q: Is this why your boyfriend now likes her?
A: Yes. That chemistry is still there, because she was his soul mate in his past life.

Q: What lesson can you get from this regression so that you can calm yourself?
A: All of it is just past experience. We feel that we like other people because of our past lives. Everything has already passed. We were born inside a different body and mind and have a different mission. Now, we have to plan for our life in the future. From this regression, I understand more that we cannot control feelings that appear in us. Those feelings are there by themselves without our intention, and that's why they will disappear by themselves.

After knowing this, we decide to continue doing nothing about those feelings. And just like waves that appear spontaneously, they will be gone without power to support them. By being static and doing nothing, we just wait until those waves disappear gradually.

In the context of the past and present life, we already die and live unaccountably. We may meet our past soul mates again in our current life. Every time we meet them again, the chemistry will still be there.

But are we going to have a relationship with them again? Are we going to collect them all as our lovers in our present life? Or are we going to make them all our soul mates

How do we know that the soul mate we choose in our life now is the best soul mate we have from the past? Aren't there many of them?

Every soul mate that has a presence in our life now only gives 25% to become our true soul mate. And 75% as the commitment that we have for this present life, commitment to learn together and have same mission; commitment to be together all the time to expand our discretions. Because, when the commitment is already planted, there will be no reason for us to be unfaithful or disloyal.

"No- actions is the best spell to deal with temptation to be unfaithful."

Chapter 12

My Wealthy Private Student Aisley

"Do your good deeds now, then you will get what you want.
Yes, it is that simple!"

When I was studying at the university, I liked to give private lesson to earn extra money. That is how I met Aisley, my private student. She was a wonderful, pretty, smart, and vibrant teenager. People just liked being around her. Her life always seemed happy and fulfilling. Since the first time I came to her house, I was amazed by her big, beautiful house. As her private teacher, I often asked to give her lesson in her room. Her bedroom was very luxurious and big. It had its own private bathroom, a special wardrobe where she kept all her clothes, and a study room.

During study breaks, Aisley often told me about her holiday time abroad with her family. On her seventeenth birthday, her parents organized a big party for her and gave her a fancy car as a present. Aisley was very close to her parents, her sister, and her brother. They looked so close and happy together. Her life was like a dream.

I've always wondered: "Why are some people born very lucky, into a wealthy family, and with understanding parents and harmony in their lives?" Some people seem to live charmed lives. I was very curious about Ainley—from material and nonmaterial perspectives. I did a self regression to see Aisley's past lives to find the causes of her wonderful life now.

Q: Can you see yourself?
A: Yes. I am wearing red shoes and knee-high socks. I have red, curly hair. I have buckled teeth, and I am acting weird, awkward, and clumsy.

Q: *Are you a girl or a boy?*
A: I am a little girl.

Q: *How old are you?*
A: Around six years old.

Q: *What's your name?*
A: Bernice. But they call me Bernie.

Q: *Where do you live and what year?*
A: Colorado, America. But the year is vague.

Q: *Okay. Let's move to few years ahead to when you are with Aisley. What do you see?*
A: I am in a hallway. It looks like a school.

Q: *What you are doing?*
A: I am sliding with a book carrier carriage. I slide very fast. I am playing around and seems like I bother lots of people. They try to avoid me; they worry that I will hit him.

Q: *How old are you?*
A: Seventeen years old.

Q: *Can you see Aisley?*
A: Oh my god! She is so pretty! Her hair is long and black. She is Bordoux. She's famous because she's pretty and elegant.

Q: *What does she do?*
A: She is walking and carrying books. She's always carrying books.

Q: Now, let's move forward to see what she does that causes her to be reborn into a wealthy and happy family. What do you see?
A: I see Bordoux walking towards her neighbor.

Q: Do you know why?
A: She teaches her neighbor every afternoon.

Q: What she's doing now?
A: There is a young boy who fell. She helps him. She treats his wound and hugs him until he stops crying...Now, she starts walking again. She finds a broken flower pot. She picks it up, cleans the mess, and puts the pot back on top of the wall. A ball hits her, but she's not mad; she's smiles and returns the ball. Now, she enters her neighbor's house.

Q: Now let's move few years ahead to see what is your biggest achievement and hers. What do you see?
A: I see a beautiful river. The princesses are relaxing on the small boat at the river. They are wearing beautiful dresses and holding embroidery umbrellas. It's a tourist attraction.

Q: What are you doing?
A: I work there as a cleaner.

Q: Is that your biggest achievement?
A: Seems like it. It's because I can do the job properly. I never make trouble anymore and drop stuff. As I told you before, I am a clumsy girl. I always irritate people with my clumsiness, and I often drop things because of my clumsy behavior. But here, I can do my job properly although people still think that I am weird.

Q: So, what is Bordoux doing now? Is she also working?
A: Bordoux works as a scientist. She might be the only female there.

Q: What kind of research she's doing?
A: Her research is about plants and their medicinal uses. She plants them in a glasshouse and then picks them. She brought them to the house where she works. That's all I know.

Q: So, what caused her to be born in a wealthy family and always been fulfilled?
A: Because she always seeks to do anything for other people. She implements what nature wants her to do. She does what she supposed to do. That is why she always gets what she wants.

Q: Can you explain that?
A: Can you see? She helped that boy, pick up the broken pot, and was not mad and even smiled when she got hit by a ball. She became a scientist to help people to find cures. She does things that nature wants her to do. She does what she supposed to do in her life. Now, she always gets what she wants. She was born in a wealthy, happy family and is loved. She has a wonderful life.

Q: So, the things you have done in the past do not qualify you to be born in a wealthy and happy family?
A: Ha ha ha...I am totally different from Bordoux. Wherever she goes, she gives happiness to people. She charms people with her good deeds. Wherever I go, I irritates other people because of my awkward behavior.

Q: Do you think that doing simple good things will give us prosperity and happiness?
A: Not simple things. We must do what we're supposed to do. We must do things that nature expects us to do. Nature wants us to do good things. If we do that, than nature will do the same thing.

Q: Is there any lesson you can get from your meeting with Aisley now?
A: Yes. I am able to see now that prosperity and wealth are good things because they came from good deeds. To become big in the next life, we have to do something amazing.
The result of this self regression makes me realize that small deeds, if continually and consciously done, will be a big beginning.

It turns out that simple things are training and preparing us to do big things. Consciousness and goodness are the seeds of prosperity in life.
If everyone knew this, that goodness will bring prosperity and everything that is good in life, then they will race to do good things in life. As if everyone can see the cause of their bad deeds, they will be frightened and stop doing it. As soon as they realize that good deeds will bring prosperity and good things, even though they are poor now, they will race to do good things. By doing so, they are actually preparing their own future life to be better.
People who were born in prosperity in their life now have to know that it's because of the good things they have done in the past. And if they can enjoy it, then they should prepare themselves for more prosperity in their future life by doing more good deeds in life.

Closing

I will end my life stories with a story titled "A Princess and A White House." Hopefully, this short story will crystallized your understanding and awareness of life characteristics and of the learning process that we go through.

One morning, there was a princess who awoke in a jungle. She didn't remember why she was there or what she was doing there. Many people surrounding her also felt that same way: they didn't know why they were there or what they were doing in that jungle.

She tried to find the answer. But the only clue she had was two sayings: "Your destination is to get to the white house. Find it and follow the path, then you fill get to the white house."

When the night came, there were howling wolves. The howls always made her suffer in pain.

One day, the princess got to a tree. On that tree, it was written: "A time tree. Because you already got this far, you can pick the fruit and see your past."

Then, the princess picked a fruit from that tree and suddenly saw herself in another jungle and in another time. She was herself, but also not herself. That princess saw a prince running from wolves' hunter. But then, those wolves captured him and he screamed.

Suddenly she was awake and that experience seemed so real. And she knew why those howls frightened her. She realized that the path that she took towards those wolves was not the right path. She had to avoid them so that they would not hunt her.

So, the princess continues her journey. She is determined to find the gate so that she doesn't have to be in that jungle anymore.

Like the princess and the people inside the story, we are all wandering in this world. That time tree is actually past lives regression (PLR) that we can use to see the causes of problems in our life that comes from our past lives. That white house symbolizes a mysterious hierarchy because a white house is a White House—and that White House is the end of the journey. Past lives regression gives us clues in this long spiritual journey.

Past lives regression has become an important and also unnecessary way to find answers for the questions in our lives. We can use or not use past lives regression to find The Path. Once we find it, the Path will guides us to our White House.

Appendix I: Script and Self Regression Technique

This is the script to see past lives that I use often. If you want to learn how to do self regression, I suggest that you record your voice from the script.

Before you study or try this self regression technique, especially first timers, I would like to explain few important things. What will someone see when they are doing past lives regression?

Someone who practices self regression will be able to view his or her past life clearly, just like watching a movie. Sometimes people just see clips or even experience relaxation, but there is always the possibility that we will experience touching moments or frightening moments. The person that having the regression will also experience fear or pain that his or her past live figure experienced that time.

Step 1: Preparation

1. Provide a room where you can concentrate during theregression process.
2. Position yourself comfortably. You can sit or lay down.
3. Clear your mind and let your mind's situation become positive.
4. Ask someone to accompany you, if you feel more comfortable that way.

Choose the most comfortable place and position for you. Make sure that you can relax. Close your eyes, get rid of every thought that bothers you, and make your body as relaxed as possible.

Step II: Relaxation

(Record this following script)

Close your eyes and relax your body. Inhale and exhale slowly. Do it one more time.

Every inhalation will make your body become more relaxed. In every exhalation, you letting go of all your worries and exhaustions. Now, you only feel your body become more relaxed and comfortable.

Then, in your mind, can see and feel a light that makes you relax. That light will make your mind more relaxed and will demolish all your worries. Now, your head becomes light and comfortable.

See and feel it, that light is going down to your face. See and feel your face become relaxed. See and feel it, that light makes your face relax.

Now, that light will go down to your throat. See and feel it, your throat tendons will be flexible and loose. See and feel it, now your throat is relaxed.

Then, the light will go down to your shoulders. See and feel it, the light will make your shoulders relaxed and comfortable. Feel your shoulders become lighter, as if you had never felt that relaxed in your shoulders before. This will makes you sleepy...and sleepier...and you will fall into deep sleep.

Now, this light will go down to both of your hands. See and feel it, your hands become relaxed and comfortable. See *and feel it, your hands' muscles become relaxed and comfortable.*

Now, this light will go down to your chest and makes your chest become relaxed and comfortable. See and feel it, that light will take away the pressures inside your chest. See and feel it, now you can breathe easily and oxygen can get through to your lungs easily. This will make you fall asleep deeply.

Then, that light will go down to your feet. See and feel it, your feet will be relaxed. See and feel it, your feet muscles will loosen up and your feet will be very relaxed.

Now, you can feel that your whole body is very relaxed. I will count from three to one. At the count of one, you will fall into a deep sleep. Three, two, one...you fall asleep deeply.

Step III: Enter your past life

(Record this following script)

Now, I want you to see and feel, you are in bright tunnel, and you feel very comfortable in that tunnel. At the end of the tunnel, there is a door; that door is the passage into your past life. I will count from three to one. At the count of one, you will be in that bright tunnel. Three...two...one...now you are in that tunnel.

I will count backward from twenty to one. At every one back count, it will rewind the time, and when I count to one, you will be in one of your past lives' moments.

Twenty....See and feel your body is moving backward in time. Nineteen...you feel relaxed and comfortable. Eighteen....your body will be light and you continue to move backward. Seventeen...rewind...rewind the time. Sixteen... fifteen....fourteen...and you become more relaxed and fall into deep sleep. Thirteen...twelve...eleven...see and feel that you're halfway through your past life. Ten...nine...eight...you become more relaxed and confident. Seven...six...you are approaching the door to your past life and you feel more relaxed. Five...you are getting closer to that door. Four...now you are already in front of the door and are ready to open it. Three...put your hand on the door handle. Two...open that door now and step to enter that door. One...you are in your past life.

Step IV: Travelling

(Record this following script. Give yourself extra time, from five to ten minutes, for every question)

Relax and comfort yourself with the view and the situation you are in now. Give yourself a couple of minutes and take a deep breath. Now see and feel your surroundings. What do you see? Can you see your own feet? Are you inside or outside? What is your name? Where are you and in what year? Let all the information and visions run through you; accept everything and everything will become crystal clear.

Three...two...one...you will be able to see your past life moments clearly.

Now you will fast forward yourself to see your biggest achievement in that past life. Three...two...one...What have you achieved in that life? Have you fulfilled your dreams? What lesson do you learn? What can you learn from that past life that you can implement in your current life?

Step V: Termination

(Record this following script)

    Now, I will count from one to five. By the fifth count, you will be awake from your regression and you will feel fresh, and you will be able to remember every moment you saw in your past life. One...feel your body become fresher. Two...See and feel that you are happier and fresher. Three...fresher and fresher...four...now be ready to be awake at the fifth count with your fresh body. Five...open your eyes and you will be awake, feeling fresh and happy.

Appendix 2: PLR Questions and Answers

My clients doing regression often ask me the following questions. Specifically, I emphasize and explain a few things related to this book's subject. Besides my own experiences and observations, I take these answers from the essence of literatures I have read on the topic.

What is the meaning of past lives regression (PLR)?

Past lives regression, by hypnosis method, is a process of doing deep relaxation to put our mind to sleep so that we can access a past life we want to see. To make it clear, please observe this picture. Try to sit relax and try to memorize your childhood. Your childhood moments will be pictured in your mind. That is the idea of simple regression, even if is not as deep as regression by hypnosis method.

What is the meaning of hypnosis?

Actually, hypnosis can be called deep relaxation. When we do hypnosis, we do relaxation to make our self consciousness sleep, so that we can access our subconscious mind. Subconscious mind is a media that stores every past, present, and even future piece of information.

How did you do PLR that resulted in what's written in this book?

In order to compile this book, I do my own PLR by doing self hypnosis and my own past lives regression. I fast forward and rewind pictures that I see from my past life, just like doing it when you are watching a movie. I develop questions, and then I get the answers from my own life's stories.

How do you do PLR?

You can do your own PLR or you can be guided by a hypnotherapist. Basically, the hypnosis process, including PLR, is self-hypnosis. A hypnotherapist only acts as interpreter and guide, but the person that has to implement and practice hypnotic process himself.

When I am being hypnotized, is my consciousness gone completely?

No, this is a common misperception. People think that when you are being hypnotized, your self consciousness vanishes and that you are totally hopeless. This is false. A person will be fully conscious, even if he is being hypnotized. He will be fully conscious of his surroundings. He cannot be forced to do things that he doesn't want to do.

When I am doing PLR, will I still be conscious?

You will be fully awake. You can hear and answer the questions that are asked by your hypnotherapist. You can memorized every detail of the hypnosis process. You also will be able to remember every detail of the past lives that you see, just like after watching a movie.

Is PLR related to mystical things or supernatural?

I know very little about the supernatural, so I don't have enough of a foundation to discuss it. PLR allows us to see our past lives when our brain is on *alpha* or *theta* frequency, because under that condition, we can access our sub-conscious mind. Our sub-conscious mind is storage for all our past, present, and future life information. We can reduce the brain frequency and reach alpha or theta frequency by putting our mind asleep. Regression, by hypnosis, uses relaxation to put our mind asleep to access our pass lives.

Can everyone do PLR?

As far as I have experienced, anyone with the determination to do self regression can succeed at PLR. It can be difficult for people who have a high levels of stress because they have trouble relaxing. You have to relax completely to do PLR, and usually after few attempts, these high-stress individuals can manage to relax enough to easily enter their past lives.

How often can I practice PLR?

There is no limit, as long as you can manage to process and take lessons from your past lives. Regression can be a cure, and it can help you develop yourself in your present life. That is the main purpose of PLR.

When is the best moment to do PLRtherapy?

You can practice past life regression when you need to get answers to questions that are impossible to answer in your present life. Those questions need to be answered so that you can continue your life in a better way.

When practicing PLR, why do I have to be guided by a hypnotherapist?

I suggest that you use a hypnotherapist for your first

PLR. A professional hypnotherapist will know how to process your regression result, and they will know what they have to do when needed. But if you cannot find a hypnotherapist that specializes in PLR, you can train yourself with a recorded script from a hypnotherapist.

To practice PLR, do I have to believe in the reincarnation concept or in being reborn?

You can believe or disbelieve it. There was a client of mine, a high school student, who didn't know those two concepts. But he was able to enter his past life, his previous life, and experience it from his death to being reborn in his mother's uterus. The main thing was that he could take valuable lesson from the regression. In the end, he gained a greater understanding of the importance of being respectful to his parents.

Is PLR against any religions?

Is there any religion that is against therapy when it is used to help people heal and develop? The answer is no. Of course you can practice this therapy. Its only function is to help in the healing process and in the self development of someone who wants to live better.

What is the basic condition to be able to implement PLR?

There are no basic rules. You just need to have the courage to see your past lives, and to get clearer and wiser in your present life.

What things can embrace PLR?

Things that can discourage someone to do PLR: mental disorder, stress, fear or hearing problem, difficult to speak and have no determination to practice PLR.

Can I trust the visions I get from PLR as true moments in my past lives?

I will answer this question with concrete example. Put a pen in front of you and then see that pen. Check how you feel in that moment. Now, hide the pen behind your back. Can you remember what you just saw? Do you still remember its color and can you picture it in your mind? Can you still remember where it was, how you felt, and in what sort of situation you saw that pen? Of course, if your mind is still properly functioning, you will be able to absorb and memorize that pen with joyful feeling and keep memories of that pen in your subconscious mind.

If you have happy memory of that pen because you remember a friend complimenting it, the next time you remember that pen, you feel happy. You can feel and memorize that same happy feeling in different time.

Can you give me more detailed explanations?

Our mind is not just responsible for keeping the image of objects that we saw. It also absorbs the feeling and the moments that happened when we saw that object. Later on, the object that we see will be trigger that will activate the feelings we have toward that object. That is why a person who drowned in the sea will feel frightened whenever he is near the sea.

Various pictures and experiences that appear during PLR come from our subconscious mind and are triggered by the questions that you have inside your mind. Pictures, experiences, feelings, and sensations are never there if you do not absorb and store them in your mind. If you cannot remember when it happens, maybe you absorbed and stored them in your past life. Those visions and experiences will help you answer your questions in PLR therapy.

How do I document my PLR results?

You could record PLR results by recording the whole process directly or you can write it when you are conscious. You will be able to remember every small detail.

Is there a way to check my PLR result documentation for its accuracy?

You can do that by checking if the lesson you received from PLR can make your life wiser, happier, more meaningful, and if it guides you to a mission. If the answer is yes, then it is true that PLR can make our life better.

Is PLR an effective way to cure mental illness?

We call it mental illness if we continue to carry the pressure and problems in our head without knowing how to release them. We hold those problems closely and that makes us sick. PLR will bring you to the problem directly and help you understand the cause of the problems that you have (your mental illness). By seeing and experiencing the cause of your problems, you will know how to release them.

Few cases of PLR therapy have helped heal physical illness. Dr. Brian Weiss client – a cancer patient who suffer cancer – became better after saw her past life. There are many cases of physical illness that become better or even cured by seeing and reviewing their past live to find out the causes of their illness. Please read *Through Time Into Healing* by Dr. Brian Weiss.

Can science support the claims of PLR?

Yes, if individuals provide supporting historical data and are able to capture the year, people's names, and places or locations, historical data often supports PLR. There was one particular unsolved murder case that was solved after implementing PLR therapy. Therapy revealed that the killer was the woman's own lover. That case was published in many American newspapers, and you can read the details in the book *Reincarnation: The Search for Grace* by Dr. Bruce Goldberg.

How should I implement lessons I learn from PLR therapy?

When you are in regression, be sure to ask specific questions about how you can apply this past life to improve your present life. The best thing you can achieve from PLR is the capability to implement the lessons you learn to live your current life with more wisdom.

Testimony

"When I enter and see my past life, it was like I was in a different world. I can feel my emotion and mood in that time. I practiced PLR to find out more about my personal relationship with someone. It turned out that there was repetitive pattern that we carrying out into our present life. After I saw my life with her in the past, I had a more objective view of our relationship. I can compare the similarity between my past and present relationship."
Paulina – *Accountant from Jakarta*

"I practiced PLR initially because I wanted to try it. I wanted to know if there was a connection between the problem that I have now and my past life, then I found out that it was closely related. I was just like I was repeating the same moment, but in a different time, place, and condition. What I was experiencing and felt in that moment was very similar to what I experiencing now. I just practiced PLR once, but I already found the source and cause of my problem. But after I knew my past life, I felt lighter and more able to accept and deal with my problem. I also tried to take a positive lesson from the past experience to find a solution so that it would not happen again in the future."
Lydia Anggariani – *Employee from Jakarta*

"Viewing my past life was just like watching a movie. I was fully conscious and recognized people who appear in my past life and in my present life. I practice PLR because I want to find my soul mate. In my past life, I can often find the source of my unsolved problems. The most important thing is that I know what steps I must take next. After I saw my past life, I

became more peaceful, confidence, and an excellent decision maker."
Alex Triadi – *Businessman from Bekasi*

"I was determined to practice PLR to see if the problems that I have now are related to my past life. The answer is no. However, when I practice PLR, I felt encouraged and knew that the solutions to my problems were already inside my mind. Because I practiced PLR, I can now make that hard decisions that I struggled with before. "
Cisca – *Housewife*

"I practice PLR because, after eight years of marriage, I am hoping for children. After getting therapy twice in October 2008 and January 2009, I found out the problem and its solution. In February 2009, I discovered that I was pregnant. My husband and the whole family were very grateful. Do not be afraid to know your past life; when we know them, we will be able to know our mistakes in the past and redeem them now."
Rita Iskandar – *Businesswoman from Jakarta*

"I practice PLR therapy with Nathalia to understand why I am such a religious person. I discovered that when I lived in China, I was a monk and taught the same religion that I am teaching now. My mum in the past is my mum now. I was a hundred years old and died peacefully. From that PLR therapy, I realized that there is no material eternity in this world. Every life has potential to develop and to improve in many aspects—and in spiritual aspects in particular."
Pierre S. – *Deputy Director SMIS*

"I respect how dedicated Nathalia is to her mission to help people to solve their problems. The PLR experience is a very interesting and unique experience for me. PLR therapy helped me gain knowledge about unbelievable dimensions. Knowing the past helps me understand more about the moments happening now. Knowing about the creation of a mission in life can give us confidence to step into the future."
Michel S - *Businessman*

"During my PLR therapy session with Nathalia, I entered my two past lives in Europe and America. I was very amazed about what I saw; everything was so real, and I really felt like I was there. In the past, I felt frozen and frightened, and in my real life, I feel the same way. I often suffered and cried. PLR therapy also answered my question about why I have always liked English—even when I was little. I also have similarities between my two past lives; in both my past lives, my mum died when I was nine."
Lim Siuk Yin – *Employee*

"I've often wondered: Is reincarnation really happening, after or before our present life? And does Karma really exist? If those things do exist, then what we can do to prove it? Through hypnosis methods, Nathalia Sunaidi has done two things that have changed my life, guiding me to enter my past life and teaching me how so that I can practice it myself. This thing has increased my belief that everything in this life happens for a reason. Nothing happens accidently. Because of karma, everything is related."
Toni Yoyo – *Speaker/ Writer/ Hypnotherapist from Tangerang*

"Through PLR therapy, I solved my relationship problem with my father. By entering different moments of my past lives, I was able to get the meaning of Karma and discretion. I also found my life's mission through this therapy."
Intan Darmawati – *Fasilitator/Trainer/Hypnotherapist from Bogor*

The Universe with all the synchronizations has brought me to meet Nathalia to practice PLR therapy. After entering my past lives, I became wiser and peaceful. I accept anything that happens in my life with an open mind. It's because now I know my life's purposes and missions. I believe more of God's will, and I am always grateful."
Fanny Fitriani – *Fashion Stylist*

"Practicing PLR is an extraordinary experience for me. PLR therapy helps me to find my life mission. I am grateful to God, because now I can find my spiritual guidance through this therapy. It turned out that the person who was always around for me is actually my spiritual guidance."
M.R. Astuty – *Employee/Hypnotherapist from Bogor*

"Since I was young, I have always believed that someone was born with happiness and sadness in life for a reason. I don't believe that God is unwise enough to give affliction to people without reason, until I met Nathalia with her PLR therapy method. Then I found out that actually life is causal and effect. Every time I practice PLR, I always learn wise message that I can use as my guide to make my life better. PLR helps me learn not to repeat the same mistakes and understand more the truly meaning of happiness—not just from money, but also from

tranquility, love, and peacefulness from inside. "
Dra. Neni Anggraeni, MM. – *Entrepreuner from Jakarta*

"Through PLR, I learn and understand more many important things than can be implemented evidently in my present life. Thanks to you, Nath."
Nana Alianto – *Housewife lives in Jakarta*

About the Author

Nathalia Sunaidi and Gunawan initially published this book in 2006 when they began the Nathalia Institute Foundation—an Institute that focuses on helping people who want to practice or learn about hypnotherapy.

Nathalia Sunaidi was born in Jakarta, January 5, 1981. Since she was young, she has always enjoyed observing the lives that surround her. Whenever her family or friends took her places, Nathalia always spent her time looking out through the window car and watching houses on the side of the streets they passed. She has always been amazed by the lives of the people inhabiting those houses. Nathalia is a sociable and friendly person. Her friends always feel comfortable sharing their stories with her, and even strangers find her easy to talk to. She is patient, empathetic, and sincere; she is also a good listener and a problem solver.

Nathalia graduated from one of the private Universities in Jakarta, majoring Computer Accounting. Psychology was her true passion, but she chose to study accounting to satisfy her parents. Even though accounting was not her first choice, she still achieved good results in the subject.

In 2002, she found a book about reincarnation and began studying the regression method of past lives (PLR) through hypnosis. Nathalia quickly comprehended the regression method and even mastered it. She began to intensify her skills in the regression method of past lives, *higher self, and future lives*.

Nathalia Sunaidi is currently the Director of the Nathalia Institute—Hypnosis Training Center and Hypnotherapy Center. She is a hypnotherapist, writer, and tutor. Though constant evaluation and thousands of hours of therapy sessions, Nathalia has expand the Wisdom Therapy method® which has been successful in her hypnotherapy sessions. She is also a member of the International Association for Regression Research and Therapy, Inc. and the National Guild of Hypnotists, USA.

Her hypnotherapy session at the Nathalia Institute has become very popular and clients are currently on a two month waiting list. Now, Nathalia also teaching a 100-hour hypnotherapy training course (Becoming a Hypnotherapist: Fundamental-Intermediate-Advanced Hypnotherapy) with an international standard curriculum at the Nathalia Institute. Through this training seminar, Nathalia educates the students to become hypnotherapists and to open their own professional hypnotherapy practices.

Nathalia is known as a hypnotherapist expert; she is also a source-speaker in seminars and talk shows in Indonesia. Her debut as a writer and a hypnotherapist has been published in *Kartini Magazine, Herworld Magazine, Ultimate Magazine, National Journal Newspaper*, Good Morning – Metro TV and Trijaya FM Radio.

To get hypnotherapy training information or to schedule therapy sessions at the Nathalia Institute, you can easily access the official website of the Nathalia Institute at www.nathaliainstitute.com. If you would like to know more about Nathalia, you can visit her site www.nathaliainstitute.com and www.nathaliasunaidi.com , find her on Facebook, or email her at nathaliasunaidi@yahoo.com.

BIBLIOGRAPHY

Andrews, Ted, *Uncover Your Past Lives,* (Jakarta: Bhuana Ilmu Populer, 2006).

Aryasura, Acharya, *Jatakamala,* (Jakarta: Bhumisambhara, 2005).

Davies, Brenda, *Journey Of The Soul,* (London: Hodder and Stoughton, 2002).

Dhammananda, K Sri, *Tumimbal Lahir: Percayakah Anda?,* (Yayasan Penerbit Karaniya, 2005).

Golberg, Bruce, *Reinkarnasi,* (Jakarta: Bhuana Ilmu Populer, 2003).

Goldberg, Bruce, *Self-Defence Against Psychic Attacks & Evil Spirits,* (New Delhi: Pustak Mahal, 1999).

Goldberg, Bruce, *Past Lives, Future Lives Revealed,* (New Jersey: Career Press, 2004).

Goldberg, Bruce, *Self Hypnosis, Revised Edition,* (New Jersey: Career Press, 2006).

Gunawan, Adi W, *Hypnosis-The art of Subconscious Communication,* (Jakarta: Gramedia Pustaka Utama, 2006).

Janakabhivamsa, Ashin, *Abhidhamma Sehari-hari,* (Yayasan Penerbit Karaniya, 2005).

Newton, Michael, *Journey Of The Souls,* (Minnesota: Llewellyn, 1994).

Newton, Michael, *Life Between Lives: Hypnotherapy For Spiritual Regression,* (Minnesota: Llewellyn, 2004).

Moody, Raymond. A, JR,M.D., *Hidup Sesudah Mati,* (Jakarta: Gramedia, 2003).

Senjaya, Andre, *Abhidhamma,* (Makalah pada kelas Abhidhamma di Ciledug, Tangerang, 2006).

Steiger, Brad, *You Will Live Again,* (Jakarta: Bhuana Ilmu Populer, 2003).

Stemman, Roy, *Reincarnation: True Stories of Past Lives,* (London: Piatkus, 2001).

Webster, Richard, *Past-Life Memories: Panduan Praktis untuk Menyingkap Kehidupan Masa Lalu,* (Jakarta: Bhuana Ilmu Populer, 2003).

Weiss, Brian, *Through Time Into Healing,* (London: Piatkus, 1998).

Weiss, Brian, *Same Soul, Many Bodies,* (London: Piatkus, 2004).

Williamson, Linda, *Finding the Spirit Within,* (London, Rider, 2001).

Nathalia institute Publishing
© 2009 Nathalia Sunaidi

www.nathaliainstitute.com
www.nathaliasunaidi.com